THE
HISTORY OF
ADVERTISING
40
MAJOR BOOKS
IN FACSIMILE

Edited by
HENRY ASSAEL
C. SAMUEL CRAIG
New York University

A
GARLAND
SERIES

ADVERTISING
AND SELLING

HARRY L. HOLLINGWORTH

GARLAND PUBLISHING, INC.
NEW YORK & LONDON
1985

659.1 H741a 1985
Hollingworth, Harry L.
Advertising and selling

For a complete list of the titles in this series
see the final pages of this volume.

This facsimile has been made from a copy in
the Library of Congress.

Library of Congress Cataloging in Publication Data

Hollingworth, Harry L.
   Advertising and selling.
   (The History of advertising)
   Reprint. Originally published: New York : D. Appleton,
c1913.
   Bibliography: p.
   1. Advertising—Psychological aspects. I. Title.
II. Series.
HF5822.H565   1985   659.1   84-46039
ISBN 0-8240-6733-9 (alk. paper)

Design by Donna Montalbano

The volumes in this series are printed on
acid-free, 250-year-life paper.

Printed in the United States of America

ADVERTISING
AND SELLING

ADVERTISING AND SELLING

PRINCIPLES OF APPEAL AND RESPONSE

BY

HARRY L. HOLLINGWORTH

INSTRUCTOR IN PSYCHOLOGY IN COLUMBIA UNIVERSITY, NEW YORK CITY; LECTURER IN
BUSINESS PSYCHOLOGY, SCHOOL OF COMMERCE, NEW YORK UNIVERSITY.

PUBLISHED FOR THE ADVERTISING
MEN'S LEAGUE OF NEW YORK CITY, INC.

D. APPLETON AND COMPANY
NEW YORK AND LONDON
1913

COPYRIGHT, 1915, BY THE
ADVERTISING MEN'S LEAGUE OF NEW YORK CITY, INC.

Printed in the United States of America

PREFACE

This book has resulted from the coöperative attempt, on the part of a group of practical business men and one or two individuals whose interests were chiefly scientific, (a) to formulate and systematize those facts and laws which relate to the processes of appeal and response in the selling and advertising of goods, and (b) to undertake investigations which might result in the discovery of new facts and principles of both practical and scientific interest. This attempt has proceeded on the basis of four distinct aims, which it is well to have clearly in mind. These aims have been:

(1) To sort out, from the general body of psychological doctrine, such principles as underlie the mental processes involved in creating, presenting and reacting to appeals which are presented in the form of advertisements, arguments, selling talks, etc.; to state these in systematic form for convenient acquisition and reference by the active and prospective business man.

(2) To examine such various methods, media and devices as have proven clearly successful or

unsuccessful in known circumstances, places, and with different commodities, and to deduce and formulate any principles revealed by such comparative study.

(3) To carry on, in a coöperative way, new experiments and investigations, by exact scientific methods, and with the definite intention of helping to render the technique of the laboratory more and more serviceable in handling the practical problems of daily business life.

(4) To devise accurate and reliable methods of testing beforehand the probable value of appeals which are intended for actual use in advertising and selling, (a) by more exact study of the known principles of appeal and response and their applications in business transactions, and (b) by a comparison of laboratory tests with keyed results produced by the appeals in business campaigns.

The results of this coöperative attempt are presented in the chapters which follow. The first line of work will constitute the skeleton of the book, and the results of the other inquiries will be introduced by way of illustration and proof of the principles presented.

The book is intended primarily for the general reader and for the student with practical rather than theoretical interests. It does not pretend to present nor even to conform to any particular "system" of academic psychology, but aspires to render more concretely serviceable, within a particular field, the accepted facts, laws and methods resulting from the experimental study of human nature and human behavior. But it is hoped that the professional student of human nature may also find the motive and method of the book to be at least suggestive, and in that sense valuable.

In its original form the book consisted of a series of lectures given, during several successive years, under the auspices of the Advertising Men's League of New York City. This fact determined the practical bearing of the material presented. It is quite impossible to give due credit to all whose work has been of service to the writer in this undertaking. From the practical point of view the suggestions and criticisms of the members and chairmen of the League Round Tables have been invaluable. On the scientific side, an attempt is made in the bibliography to indicate the chief sources which have been specifically utilized. But I must render particular thanks to the many members of my college classes whose zeal and labor have made many of the experiments possible. I am under especial obligation to Dr. E. K. Strong, Jr., at one time assistant in the Barnard laboratory, and since Research Fellow, in Columbia University, for the

Advertising Men's League and the National Association of Advertising Managers, for his constant interest and assistance, and for a great amount of data, more specifically referred to in the text.

But, above all, the very existence of the book, the opportunity of preparing it, and very much of such concreteness and value as the book may contain are due to the untiring activity and the stimulating professional ideals of Mr. Wm. H. Ingersoll, President of the Advertising Men's League. It was under his leadership that the Round Table Study Course was conceived and effectually organized, and through his suggestions and advice that the course on Principles of Appeal and Response was originally planned.

HARRY L. HOLLINGWORTH.

Columbia University,
      New York.

CONTENTS

CHAPTER	PAGES
I.—Measuring the Strength of an Appeal Machinery Advertisements—Soap Advertisements—Electric Light Advertisements.	1–16
II.—The Nervous Basis of Mental Processes	17–27
III.—The Analysis of Task and Media . . . The Task — Analysis of Advertising Types—Media.	28–45
IV.—The First Task: Catching the Attention Causes of Attention—Results and Laws of Attention.	46–59
V.—Mechanical Incentives . . . . Intensity — Magnitude — Motion — Contrast—Isolation—Position.	60–90
VI.—Interest Incentives . . . . Novelty—Color—Cuts and Illustrations—Suggested Activity—The Comic—Feeling Tone, Instinct and Habit.	91–126
VII.—An Experimental Test of the Relative Attention and Memory Value of the Mechanical and Interest Devices . .	127–131
VIII.—The Second Task: Holding the Attention Mechanical Helps—Interest Devices.	128–141
IX.—Feeling Tone of Form . . . . Lines—Closed Forms—Principles of Design.	142–157

CONTENTS

CHAPTER	PAGES
X.—FEELING TONE OF CONTENT	158–188

Character of Colors—Color Combinations—Color Balance—Feeling Tone and Imagination—Strain and Relaxation.

XI.—THE THIRD TASK: FIXING THE IMPRESSION . . . 189–215
Principles of Connection—Laws of Original Connection—Principles of Revival—Minor Devices—Memorability of Different Kinds of Facts—Trade Marks—Vicarious Sacrifices in Advertising.

XII.—THE FOURTH TASK: PROVOKING THE RESPONSE 216–236
Direct Appeals to Feeling—The Nature and Laws of Suggestion—The Laws of Suggestion.

XIII.—INSTINCTS, THEIR NATURE AND STRENGTH . 237–252

XIV.—THE RELATIVE STRENGTH OF THE CHIEF INSTINCTS AND INTERESTS 253–286
Summary.

XV.—SEX AND CLASS DIFFERENCES OF INTEREST TO BUSINESS MEN 287–305
Sex Differences—Age and Class Differences.

BOOKS AND ARTICLES REFERRED TO IN THE TEXT OR RECOMMENDED FOR FURTHER READING 306

LIST OF ILLUSTRATIONS AND DIAGRAMS

	PAGES
Machinery advertisements	6, 7
Soap advertisements	12, 13
A long circuit appeal	23
A short circuit appeal	25
A classified appeal	32
Publicity appeal	34
Publicity appeal	34
Display appeal	36
Display appeal	37
Forms of focal points of attention	47
An experiment on attention	57
Graphite advertisements	68, 69, 70
White on black	77
Attention value of isolation	79
Absence of counter attraction	80
Novelty as an effective attention device	93
The conventional	94
The novel	95
Curves showing visual acuity with lights of different colors	97
Chromatic aberration in the human eye	104
Illustration as an attention and interest device	106
The use of illustration	107
A strictly relevant illustration	110

LIST OF ILLUSTRATIONS AND DIAGRAMS

PAGES

An irrelevant illustration........................111
A remotely relevant illustration.................111
Irrelevant illustration 112
Violating the law of the resting point............116
Illustrating the law of the resting point.........117
The objective comic. The calamity..............121
The objective comic. The naïve..................122
The subjective comic. Play on words............123
The subjective comic. Play on words............124
Influence of repetition on the objective comic....125
Influence of repetition on the subjective comic....126
Figures appearing to change character...........134
Cards from New York Subway...................135
Securing unity through structure................136
An attempt to secure unity by mechanical means..138
The fine black line, suggesting precision and hardness 143
The broad black line, suggesting solidity and weight 144
Appropriate use of horizontal lines..............145
Inappropriate use of diagonal lines..............146
Feeling tone from direction of lines..............148
Rhythm in design..........................152, 153
Balance of mass against vista....................155
Mechanical balance of mass against mass.......155
The law of balance disregarded..................156
Harmonious coördination of subject, type and trade mark 167
Type faces suggesting refinement and delicacy of the texture 167
Inappropriate feeling tone.......................174
Feeling tone of associations inappropriately used..175
Strain 178

LIST OF ILLUSTRATIONS AND DIAGRAMS

PAGES

Relaxation 179
Use of lower case letters and of favorable length of line......................................180
Illegibility resulting from the exclusive use of capital letters 182
Illegibility and strain is produced by too great variety of type faces, interrupted lines and ineffective spacing 183
Illustrating the ease of reading and feeling of relaxation produced by the use of lower case letters and by the presence of appropriate spacing 184
Forward reasoning—correct arrangement........194
Backward reasoning—incorrect arrangement.....195
The curve of forgetting........................203
Relative attention value of fifty geometrical forms.213
General and specific appeals.......240, 241, 242, 243

PRINCIPLES OF APPEAL AND RESPONSE

CHAPTER I

MEASURING THE STRENGTH OF AN APPEAL

One of the first tasks of any science is that of devising methods of measurement. There could be no science of physics without the possibility of measuring forces, velocities, magnitudes, temperatures, etc. Experimental psychology arose only when men began to succeed in measuring the intensity, speed, uniformity and difference of mental and motor processes. In so far as salesmanship is to be scientific it must also evolve methods of measuring its materials.

Now the first step in any business transaction is the presentation of what we may call, for the sake of convenience and simplicity, an *appeal*. This appeal may take the form of an advertisement, an informal selling talk, or a more direct proposition such as a form or personal letter or circular, or it may consist merely in the knowledge, on the part of the customer, that a given commodity possesses certain desirable qualities, will accomplish certain results, etc. It will be seen at once that all salesmen are not equally persuasive, all advertisements are not equally effective, nor are all qualities or results equally valuable. A question of prime importance, then, is: "How is it possible to determine the strength, the 'pulling power' of an appeal?" If such measurement is possible, this will be the first step in the application of scientific method to this field.

It is, of course, obvious that the relative strength of appeals may be measured by the determination of the actual results: the number of inquiries, the amount of sales, the cost per sale, the demand for the articles, etc. Attempts to make these measurements have always been made. The sales of each salesman have been checked up with those of others, advertisements have been keyed, by means of different addresses, street or box numbers, differently numbered catalogues, etc. The effects of changes in location, new methods of display, etc., have been judged by the subsequent changes in output. But two difficulties in the use of these methods are apparent at once.

MEASURING STRENGTH OF AN APPEAL

In the first place it is exceedingly difficult to trace, with any precision, the actual effect of an appeal already presented. Innumerable disturbing factors complicate the calculation: the season, the medium, the activities of competitors and imitators, the method of sale (whether retail, wholesale, mail order, etc.), the effects of other means of publicity which may be operating at the same time, changes in styles, wants, and general prosperity on the part of consumers. Conditions are not under control and even inferior methods may occasionally be more remunerative, for the time being, than a more cautious attempt to secure the uniform conditions of trade, circulation, competition, etc., which would be required for a careful experimental measurement.

The second difficulty is that such methods are costly. All the measurements take place *after* the appeal has been presented, and expenses must be met regardless of the success or failure of the appeal. Coöperation might afford relief at this point were it not for two facts. The results of one campaign involving one commodity, one clientele, one set of executive and distributive operations, cannot be carried over bodily to another business venture in which all or several of these factors are changed. Further, business is competitive, and successful methods are not proclaimed and communicated to all comers.

We must devise, then, not only a method of measurement, but a method which will permit of measurement *beforehand,* and which will be so flexible as to permit adaptation to widely variant circumstances. And since we are dealing with such subjective things as interest, feelings, persuasions, attention, choice, motive, action, belief, we cannot employ any objective scale such as the yard stick, the balance, the clock work, or thermometer. But we need not despair. In the psychological laboratory we find students measuring the intensity of sensations, the degree of attention, the strength of belief, the legibility of handwriting, the agreeableness of color combinations, the excellence of literary compositions, the eminence of scientific men, the humor of comic situations, and many other things which are no less subjective than the persuasiveness of a selling talk or the pulling power of an advertisement. It was in such a laboratory that the first successful attempt was made to measure beforehand the relative strength of such appeals as are commonly employed in business. In the following portions of this chapter descriptions will be given of some of these measurements, which were made in my own laboratory, either by myself or by my students and fellow workers. In later chapters the various methods employed will be presented, and I shall further show how the application of such laboratory methods enables us not only to measure the strength of the appeal as a whole, but also to analyze it into its various elements. By means of such analysis we can determine the nature of these elements, the ways in which people of various ages and classes react to them, the deeper-lying reasons for these reactions, and can present in concrete detail the processes going on in the mind of the customer engaged in a business transaction.

In the following accounts the general plan will be:

1. To secure measurements, by laboratory methods, of the probable relative values of various appeals. In doing this we must arrange for controlled conditions by restricting the appeals to the same commodity or type of article, and by keeping uniform, for the time being, such items as size, legibility, familiarity, etc. These factors will later be discussed, each in its proper place.

2. Having measured the appeals in the laboratory, we shall secure the actual returns or re-

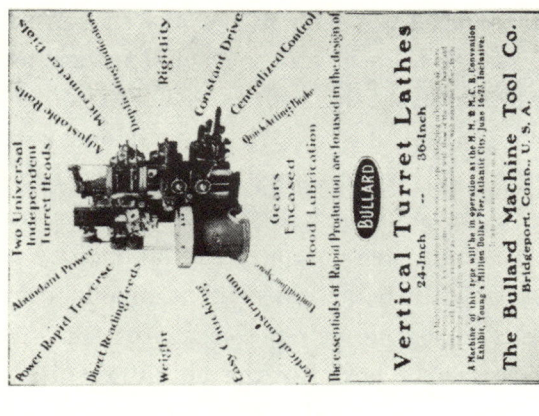

sults which the appeals produced. Partly for this reason printed advertisements are chosen as material rather than letters, personal interviews, or the commodities themselves. The results will, however, apply as well to the various sorts of appeal already enumerated in so far as they have elements in common with the advertisement.

3. We shall then compare the laboratory measurements with the actual returns provided by the business concerns using the advertisements, in order to see in how far the actual results after circulation agree with the laboratory results which could have been determined beforehand. In no case were the actual results revealed until the laboratory measurements had been already made and announced.

MACHINERY ADVERTISEMENTS

The first series studied was a set of machinery advertisements shown in the illustrations on pp. 6 and 7. There are five appeals, of uniform size, each constituting an attempt to influence buyers or inquirers in favor of the same commodity. The following table shows the results of the laboratory test, the ten persons experimented on being seniors in an engineering school, thus represent-

MEASURING STRENGTH OF AN APPEAL

ing the general class of people to whom such appeals would be directed in the natural course of business. If a given appeal was found to be the strongest for a given individual, it was marked 1 for him. If it was found to be the least persuasive, it was marked 5, and the intermediate positions indicate corresponding places in the order of strength. In the final column of the table is given the actual order of merit of these five advertisements, determined by the number of inquiries which followed upon each when run in the same medium. It is not necessary at this point to discuss two factors which will at once occur to the mind of every business man: the "cumulative effect" of successive appeals, and the "law of diminishing returns" which may operate when a series of appeals is presented to the same body of readers. These factors will be treated in their

TABLE I

Appeal	Ten different persons tested	Average	Order of Superiority by test	Order of Superiority by actual returns
A	4 3 2 3 2 3 4 4 4 1	3.0	4	4
B	5 5 1 4 5 1 1 1 1 2	2.6	2	2
C	1 1 3 1 4 2 2 2 3 4	2.3	1	1
D	2 4 5 5 3 5 5 5 5 5	4.4	5	5
E	3 2 4 2 1 4 3 3 2 3	2.7	3	3

PRINCIPLES OF APPEAL AND RESPONSE

proper places. They do not influence the significance of the returns in the case now under consideration.

If now the relative values of these appeals, as judged by actual inquiries produced, be compared with the order as determined by laboratory tests, it will be seen that the two orders agree perfectly. The tests showed C to be the strongest and D to be the weakest, and, as a matter of fact, C pulled forty times as many inquiries as did D, in spite of the fact that the cost of running and preparing D was six times as great as for C. The other appeals range between these two extremes. The testing of this series in the laboratory before their appearance would have resulted in the elimination of the weaker appeals, and consequently in increase of returns and diminution in the cost of publicity. The reasons for the striking differences in the strength of these five appeals will be made clear in subsequent chapters. Analysis leads to the discovery of differences and of principles which are true not only for the appeals in this series but for appeals in general. The point to be made now is that the laboratory test is a genuine and reliable measure of the pulling power of the different advertisements.

MEASURING STRENGTH OF AN APPEAL

SOAP ADVERTISEMENTS

A second case of close agreement is shown in Table II. The series of appeals consisted of eight advertisements. Two laboratory tests were made, one on 25 people, and the other on a different group of 100 people. The advertisements are shown on pp. 12 and 13. The first column in the table gives the letters used to identify the advertisements. The second column shows the relative persuasiveness of the appeals as determined by the first experiment, the third column as determined by the second experiment. These two tests

TABLE II

Appeal	Result of First Experiment	Result of Second Experiment	As judged by Pack'r Mf. Co.	As judged by Advt. Agency
A	1	2	4	2
B	2	1	1	3
C	3	3	2	1
D	4	4	3	4
E	5	5	5	5
F	6	6	6	6
G	7	7	7	7
H	8	8	8	8

agreed perfectly except that advertisement A, which stood first in pulling power in the first test, stood second in the second test. The fourth column gives the relative order of merit of the ap-

A

B

C

D

E

F

G

H

PRINCIPLES OF APPEAL AND RESPONSE

peals, as judged by the manufacturing company concerned, on the basis of twenty years' experience. The final column gives the order as judged by three experts of the advertising agency which had charge of this firm's publicity campaigns. Each of these various orders was determined independently, and without knowledge of the results of the other orders. The agreement is almost as striking as it was in the case of the machinery appeals. A change in the grading of just one advertisement in each of the last three columns will make all four columns agree. It is apparent that a preliminary laboratory measurement affords real knowledge of the strength of such appeals.

ELECTRIC LIGHT ADVERTISEMENTS

A third example must suffice by way of merely illustrating the reliability of the laboratory measurement. Table III shows five electric light advertisements as measured first by laboratory test and second by the cost per inquiry produced. Appeals A and B are the best two by both measurements. On appeals C and D the two measurements agree within one place in the series. Only on E is there any considerable discrepancy.

MEASURING STRENGTH OF AN APPEAL

TABLE III

Appeal	Order as measured by cost per inquiry	Order as measured by laboratory test
A	1	2
B	2	1
C	3	4
D	4	5
E	5	3

Many significant things are revealed in these experiments which enable us to formulate general laws as well as to test the value of the specific appeals. By way of illustration, it must suffice for the present to call attention to appeal B in the first experiment, that with the machinery advertisements. Notice that in Table I, where the measurements of each of the ten people are recorded, B stands either at the top or at the bottom of the series of five appeals—never in the middle. Except for two people this appeal stands either first or last, and these two exceptions are not real differences, for even here the positions are 2 and 4. This means that there are two types of people in the group studied. For one type appeal B is very effective, and these are, be it noted, the very people for whom appeal D is very weak. For the other group, for whom appeal B is weak, D is fairly strong. Each of these appeals B and

PRINCIPLES OF APPEAL AND RESPONSE

D, then, influences only one-half of the group of people. To secure a more universal appeal it would be necessary either to run both advertisements, thus doubling the cost of returns, or to construct a third type of appeal which should combine the virtues of B and D. Appeal C is as close an approximation to this ideal appeal as the series affords. Note that it stands fairly high for both types of people. Only in two cases does it stand below the middle of the series. These differences are not accidental nor peculiar to this series of appeals. They are found in many series and with every group of people I have had occasion to study. Explanation of these facts will be given in due time.

CHAPTER II

THE NERVOUS BASIS OF MENTAL PROCESSES

Every mental process, even that of being impressed or repelled by an advertisement or a salesman, has a nervous basis. We have many proofs of this dependence of consciousness upon the nervous system. Thus injuries to the nervous system affect our consciousness, as do drugs which act temporarily upon the nerve tissue. Many forms of mental disease are caused by destructive processes in the nervous system. Experimental physiology finds that certain areas in the brain are control centers for certain sets of movements and of higher sensory and mental processes such as seeing, hearing, understanding the meaning of words, associating ideas, etc. All of our knowledge depends on the possession of sense organs—eye, ear, etc., and these sense organs are only special modifications of parts of the nervous system. Finally, comparative anatomy shows us that in the animal series, from lowest to highest forms, increase in the complexity

PRINCIPLES OF APPEAL AND RESPONSE

of consciousness is always accompanied by increased complexity of the nervous system.

Consequently, any study of mental processes should take account, also, of the underlying nervous processes. Such an account not only aids greatly in the explanation of the mental processes, but also serves as a scheme or diagram which is useful in systematizing and remembering the mental processes themselves, their laws, and their relations to each other.

Considered from this point of view a man is simply a nervous mechanism, which is capable, on the one hand, of being sensitive to objects and events in the outside world, and, on the other hand, of responding to these impressions by the various sorts of movements which make up his reactions, his behavior. Sensation on the one hand and movement on the other, sum up his life. When the sense impression is very simple—a sound, or a flash of light—we call it a *stimulus;* when it is more complex—an invitation, a problem, a strange object, an argument or an advertisement—we call it an *appeal*. When the reaction is very simple we call it a *movement;* when it is more complicated, and perhaps involves many movements, we call it a *response*.

All mental life, then, can be analyzed into the

two simple elements of *appeal* and *response.* A motorman suddenly sees a danger signal and stops his car. The red light is the appeal, and his movement in applying the brakes is the response. We try to teach a child to talk. The object we point to is the appeal, his speech movements are his response. Even the little politenesses and civilities of social life, the conventionalities of the street, the seashore, the banquet table, are solely a matter of this or that response to this or that situation. What distinguishes the insane man from the rest of us is the fact that he responds wrongly or irregularly to the stimuli and appeals of the world in which he is placed.

In salesmanship the situation is quite the same. Given a certain salesman, a certain article, a certain set of advantages or arguments, this constitutes the *appeal.* The important factor remaining is the way in which the customer will *respond* to the given appeal. The operation of an advertisement, be it good or bad, is precisely the same process. The appeal here usually comes through the sense of sight; it consists, let us suppose, of a poster of definite size, position, color and composition, and it advances certain selling points for the article it desires to announce. Here is the sensory side, the stimulus. Now how does the

PRINCIPLES OF APPEAL AND RESPONSE

passerby react to the appeal? It may "catch his eye," he may read it through, and, either now or on a later occasion, buy the article. Or he may behave quite differently. The appeal may never come into his consciousness, in which case the poster is passed unnoticed. Or he may observe it, remark, "What a glaring, unsightly blotch of color!" and pass by on the other side. No matter which of these things he does, it constitutes his response—a response made up of movement and general behavior.

A pertinent question now is: What is the nervous mechanism of such a process; what happens in the nervous system when a man responds to a stimulus? Here, then, we must get some knowledge of the nervous elements, and some insight into the way in which these elements combine to form the complex nervous system.

The simplest nervous mechanism that can underlie a process of appeal and response is a combination of two nerve cells. These cells are minute structures with a main body and two sets of branches. The cells are situated for the most part in the brain and in or alongside the spinal cord. There are, in the main, two kinds of nerve cells, sensory cells and motor cells. The sensory cell sends one long branch out to the surface of the body to some sense organ, as the eye, ear, finger tips, etc. The other branches of this cell are short, and run chiefly toward motor cells which lie at a greater or less distance from it in the brain or cord. These short branches are met by the short processes coming from the motor cell, which in turn sends its long fiber out to a muscle, in some more or less remote part of the body.

This arrangement constitutes what is known as a "reflex arc," because nervous impulses pass along it much as do electrical currents along a circuit. Nervous energy set up by the outside stimulus passes along the sensory fiber to the center, where it is transmitted to the motor cell and passed on out to the muscle, reinforced, perhaps, by energy from other cells that are acting at the same time. The result is a movement of the muscle. The response is caused directly, we may even say mechanically, by the energy generated by the stimulus. So the nervous element falls into two sections, a *sensory end which is the basis of appeal,* and *a motor end which is the basis of response.*

These pure reflexes are not usually accompanied by consciousness. The impulse simply passes into the spinal cord and out. Examples

PRINCIPLES OF APPEAL AND RESPONSE

of such reflexes are blinking the eye when struck at, sneezing, coughing, the heart beat, etc.

But this simple arc represents the lowest level of nervous activity, that controlled by spinal centers. In the human being we may point out two higher and more complicated levels, which involve in the one case the higher brain, or cerebrum, and in the other the lower brain area, the cerebellum, medulla, etc.

Thus some appeals do not lead to an immediate and reflex response, but require deliberation, comparison and choice. These higher thought processes, processes of reasoning, argument, and decision, depend on the activity of nervous centers in the cerebrum. The sensory impulse, instead of issuing from the cord at once, in the form of a motor impulse, passes over a more devious path. It runs up along the cord to the higher brain centers and sets up activity through processes which, on the side of consciousness, appear as memories, associations, trains of thought, judgments. Only after these processes have been brought to bear on the appeal, when the past experience, conscious knowledge, interests, purposes, and ideals have determined what sort of response should most profitably follow—only then does the reaction come. What the response will be, or when it will come, can not be predicted from the outside, as was the case with the simple reflexes. The response may be delayed, its character is uncertain, and it may be quite out of proportion to the physical strength of the stimulus.

A Long Circuit Appeal

Such a process of appeal and response operates, we may say, by means of *the higher level*. It involves what we may call in the psychology of advertising and salesmanship *the long circuit*. It is apparent at once that it corresponds to a well-known type of selling talk, the *reason why* copy which invites and presents careful comparisons and weighing of advantages and disadvantages, copy which consists of the candid exposition of *selling points*.

But there are objects in our experience which, although they do not provoke an immediate reflex response, are, nevertheless, reacted to much more quickly, uniformly, and strongly than those which operate over the *long circuit*. Thus, in looking over a book catalogue there are certain titles which immediately catch my attention and lead me to examine them closely. Other titles I may seem not to see. If I am out walking on a fine afternoon and see a baseball game in progress in a nearby field, I find myself stopping to watch it, quite as a matter of course and with no preliminary deliberation. If I am passing through a lonesome part of the city on a dark night and see a stealthy form slink behind a tree ahead of me, I *instinctively* reach toward my hip pocket or tighten my grip on my walking stick. So when the mother sees an advertisement that offers an article guaranteed to promote baby's comfort, or when an ambitious man sees a device described that will certainly economize his time or otherwise increase his efficiency, he finds that, quite in an unpremeditated way, he has left off doing other things and is reading through the announcement or description. All of these responses, while perhaps not immediate, are, nevertheless, quick; they are strong, and we can be reasonably

A Short Circuit Appeal

certain in advance what their character will be. We will find that in such cases the object has appealed to some universal *instinct, interest* or *de-*

sire, or has awakened some strong *feeling.* Such appeals call into action centers which are prompt, powerful and definite in their response. Such a process, then, involves what we may call the *short circuit.* Such an appeal obviously, in turn, corresponds to a distinct kind of argument, the *display advertisement* or the emotional selling talk which does not argue but simply attempts to work on strong feeling, instinct or ideal. The range of such special appeals is exceedingly wide, for there are many objects in our experience toward which we all react by this *feeling* circuit, without stopping to ask why we so respond. Our reaction is determined beforehand, for the most part by the history of the race in dealing with these objects.

Generally speaking, it is true that the long circuit is determined chiefly by the past experience of the individual, the short circuit by the history of the race. All of us behave in both ways. The particular way in which we respond on a given occasion will depend on the character of the appeal, the commodity concerned, the type of the person, his age, sex, present activity, and a great number of other individual differences which it is the business of psychology to study, classify and explain.

NERVOUS BASIS OF MENTAL PROCESSES

The practical value of a study of human nature comes to depend on the fact that there are some *universals,* some ways in which all people are alike. When no such universal traits are found, there will be either types or classes, the members of which resemble each other, or the members of the race will be distributed according to a more or less bilaterally symmetrical curve, with the greatest number of individuals arranged about the average or central type, while others depart from this type both above and below, the number of people for a given character becoming less the further that character is from the type.

Here, then, is a concrete problem in salesmanship and advertising. For what sort of commodities and with what sort of people is the direct short circuit appeal effective; what objects and classes of objects can be effectively advertised and sold by an appeal to special feelings or instincts? And for what objects will the long circuit be employed, the *reason why* argument, most effectively? Some answer to these questions we may hope to get as we continue, answers based partly on our general psychological knowledge, partly on the concrete experience of practical men and partly on definite experiments now being performed in the laboratories.

CHAPTER III

ANALYSIS OF TASK AND MEDIA

THE TASK

We may analyze the task of an argument or an advertisement in terms of the reflex arc, for their operation is the same as the operation of any other stimulus. The process is always:

1. Stimulus catches attention, comes to notice, separates itself from other impressions.
2. The impression either (a) at once drops out of consciousness, or (b) holds the attention, i.e., becomes dominant in consciousness and causes adjustment of the perceiving organ for closer examination.
3. In so doing it arouses central associations, memories, interests, feelings, and becomes firmly attached to these; the impression is fixed, and remains as idea or image.
4. It leads to motor response. This response

ANALYSIS OF TASK AND MEDIA

is an essential factor in determining the final meaning of the appeal. Psychologically as well as commercially, the response is one of the most important elements in the whole process.

Always bear in mind that a sensory impression or revived image has its inevitable motor issue. This will be an important principle later on. We shall only mention it now. And remember that this response does much to determine the *character of the perception*. Observe this process when a fly lights on the baby's cheek, or when we run a sliver in our finger:

1. We say: "Oh! what's that? Oh! it's a sliver."
2. We carefully observe the sliver, locate it, observe its length, depth, etc.
3. By the *short circuit* we respond at once by instinctive movements, sucking, grimacing, pressing, etc.
4. By the *long circuit* we compare, remember, reflect, and either secure a jackknife or go to a doctor.
5. We remember the event and act more quickly next time by virtue of this mem-

PRINCIPLES OF APPEAL AND RESPONSE

ory and response. The object is characterized by the response.

An advertisement must go through the same process:

1. I see Ingersoll's watch advertisement with the many hands. I say: "Hello, what's that?"
2. I examine it, read it through with care.
3. But now comes the apparent difference between the advertisement and the ordinary stimulus. With the ordinary stimulus the response, we may think, is immediate. But it is not always. With lower forms of life this is true. But the chief difference between man and lower forms is in the retarded reaction. Even the response to a pin prick may be delayed and complicated. Such delay usually characterizes the response to an advertisement, and this constitutes one of the two chief psychological differences between *advertising* and *salesmanship*. Hence the impression must be fixated for delayed response, must be remembered, and given, in memory, preference over other advertisements for similar commodities.

ANALYSIS OF TASK AND MEDIA

4. Finally the appeal must lead to specific response, to favorable action toward the particular article or brand announced.

This analysis gives us the psychological tasks of an appeal. It will be advantageous to preface our study of these four tasks with a brief examination of the pure psychology involved in these four aspects of the reflex are:

1. In the first section we have to do with the psychology of *attention* and *perception.*
2. In the second with the psychology of *attention, interest,* and *feeling,* etc.
3. In the third with the psychology of *memory, association, emotion, mental imagery,* etc.
4. Lastly with *volition, habit, instinct, effective conception, imitation, suggestion,* etc.

Before taking up the investigation of these four fundamental sections, we may with profit get a general view of advertisements in their different forms, see what the general psychological character of each type is, and inquire in which forms the psychological subtleties play a rôle, and in which they do not. Let us first examine the appeal with respect to its own purpose and charac-

PRINCIPLES OF APPEAL AND RESPONSE

ter, and then with respect to the medium in which it is found, for media as well as individual advertisements have their psychology.

ANALYSIS OF ADVERTISING TYPES

With respect to their quality and purpose, we may distinguish three chief types of advertisements.

I. *The Classified Advertisement.*—Here the psychological subtleties play their feeblest rôle.

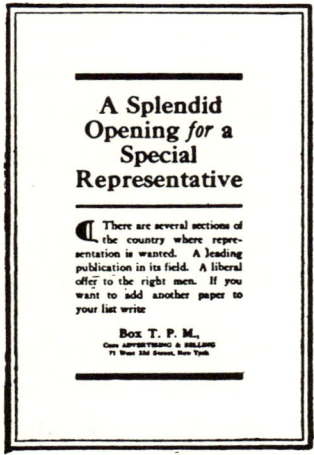

A CLASSIFIED APPEAL

The classified advertisement contains a simple announcement or invitation, intended only for those who are *a priori* interested in it. It will be sought

ANALYSIS OF TASK AND MEDIA

for by the proper person. In fact, you would rather the other person did not see it. His correspondence would only annoy you. You already have attention and interest. You need not seek for mnemonic qualities, for the right person will surely make a memorandum of the matter. You will have no difficulty in provoking response. The right person will respond without further incentive. The only psychology involved here is the psychology of intelligibility. We must observe:

1. The psychology of expression—of clear, accurate and succinct statement—and this chiefly as a means of eliminating the wrong correspondent.
2. The ordinary psychology of typography—the laws of reading, spacing, position, cataloging, color, legibility of type, etc.
3. The knowledge of media, which is not so much a matter of *a priori* psychology as a matter of advertising technology and statistics. This is a separate field in the science of business in which there is yet much to be done.

II. *The Publicity Advertisement.*—This type is not, strictly speaking, an advertisement at all, i.e., it does not pretend to operate successively on

PRINCIPLES OF APPEAL AND RESPONSE

NATIONAL BISCUIT COMPANY GRAHAM CRACKERS
—10¢—
A PACKAGE

PUBLICITY APPEAL

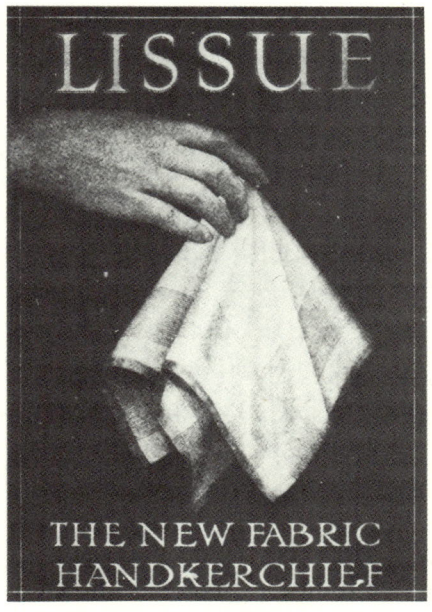

LISSUE

THE NEW FABRIC HANDKERCHIEF

PUBLICITY APPEAL

ANALYSIS OF TASK AND MEDIA

the complete arc. It is a public reminder, intended to reinforce informative appeals already issued or about to come. It usually seeks merely to familiarize a name or trade mark already known, or excite curiosity concerning a commodity about to be announced.

(1) Its psychology is usually mechanical—utilizing the principles of *size* and *contrast.*

(2) Its mnemonic psychology is also mechanical, utilizing chiefly the principle of *repetition.*

(3) But it also involves the psychology of *names,* that of *trade marks* and that of *the memorability of different kinds of facts.*

III. *Display Advertisements.*—In display advertisements the rôle of psychological factors is most prominent. The display advertisement explicitly takes the place of the salesman; it is a direct appeal, and is calculated to provoke a more or less direct, and more or less immediate response. According to its kind, it may work through the rational circuit or the feeling circuit. All parts of the arc are thus involved. It is consequently on this type of advertisement that we will base most of our analysis, chiefly because of its ideal character. But all that is said of this

DISPLAY APPEAL

type will be seen to apply in greater or less degree to the two other types, and to all forms of business appeal which have elements in common with advertisements.

ANALYSIS OF TASK AND MEDIA

Display Appeal

MEDIA

With respect to media, we may briefly summarize the chief psychological characteristics, if only for the sake of having them stated. Every business man knows the points in a more or less defined way, and, indeed, with much more certainty than I do. But you will always find knowledge clarified by an attempt at expression. Expression discloses fallacies, shows up vague spots, and crystallizes truth.

We may roughly distinguish eight classes of media. The list is not complete in this day of multitudinous publicity devices, but the classes may roughly cover the field. Briefly, these classes are as follows, classified according to psychological character and situation:

I. *Newspapers, Magazines, Periodicals, Trade Journals.*—Here the appeal is more or less incidental to other matter contained in the medium. Everybody reads, and while reading may happen upon the advertisement. But the *essential* part of the medium is the other content. Generally speaking, if the appeal is to compete with this matter, it must vie with it in attractiveness and interest.

> 1. Studies (see Scott) of 2,000 *newspaper* readers show this to be especially true here. One-half of these Chicago men, from all ranks, read two papers daily, one-fourth of them read three, while 10% read as many as four. The average time spent on these papers daily is 10-15 minutes, though many people spend as much as two

ANALYSIS OF TASK AND MEDIA

hours. Only 4%, indeed, spent less than 15 minutes, while 25% spent more.

That news is the chief item of interest in papers is also indicated by Scott's table in which about 70% of interest goes to *news,* and only one-half of 1% *explicitly* to advertisements.

Obviously the successful newspaper advertisement must in some way compete with *news interest*. The classified advertisement does this successfully, for it is in itself an item of news to those for whom it is intended. This type of appeal, then, is psychologically adapted for newspaper insertion.

> 2. The display advertisement can, then, increase its power by becoming newsy. This point has already been emphasized by Kennedy in his chapter on "Advertising is News." This idea, again, is of course the basis of the well-known success of the Wanamaker news sheet in the dailies. The more the advertisement resembles *news* in its tone, the better it will compete in interest with other news items. The success of this competition is well illustrated by an incident which I quote on the authority of Edwin Balmer, who says in

"Science of Advertising": "One of the Philadelphia newspapers, which had published Wanamaker's advertisements for years, lost 20,000 circulation when the advertisement was withdrawn, and regained it again when the department store's patronage returned" (p. 20). It does not necessarily follow from what I have just said that newspaper advertising should imitate the form and style of news paragraphs. This would be too much like the old trick advertisements that began with some startling declaration which read like a news item but wound up by extolling Somebody's Bitters or Corn Salve. Advertising that attracts by deception is psychologically vicious. The point here is simply that newspaper advertisements should be informative in character, that they should really convey interesting news of stock, prices, styles, location, changes, sales, etc. The newspaper is thus specially adapted for local advertising.

3. The value of *magazines* as a medium is high, but of course depends both on the character of the magazine and on that of the subscription list. Scott observed 600

men in the Chicago public library, noticing what part of the periodical they were reading at the moment observed. He found $10\frac{1}{2}\%$ of these men reading advertisements, and remarks that probably few did not look at the advertising pages before leaving. A prominent advertising expert, knowing the Chicago library, remarks that these results are not typical of general circulation, that libraries are always full of loafers who never buy and seldom read, but who come in to pass away the time by looking at the pictures. Concerning trade journals, little need be said. Appeals here much resemble classified advertisements. They reach a selected class of readers, those for whom they are intended, and are often, by this very fact, full of news interest of a business kind.

II. *Circulars, Hand Bills, Posters, Bulletin Boards, Electric Signs, Placards and Signs in Street Cars.*—The news interest is largely absent here, and for two reasons:

1. There is no news interest to be contended with.

PRINCIPLES OF APPEAL AND RESPONSE

2. Their size or duration forbids the news interest type for lack of space or time.

For such media the *publicity appeal* is hence psychologically adapted with its simple purpose and mechanical method. Perhaps the chief exception is to be found in the case of car advertisements. In the average city, each inhabitant, it is said, averages 10 minutes daily in street cars. As to number of people—in 1902, five thousand million cash fares were collected from passengers on street cars in the United States, besides passes and transfers. For the past year the New York subway averaged over 1,000,000 passengers daily.

Appeals here have longer time to impress themselves than in papers and magazines, and the average passenger is unoccupied. Hence, there is not so much need of devices for *catching* attention, and more room for use of logic, persuasion, affirmation, beauty, etc., than in other places. But there is more need of devices for *holding* attention because of competing cards. The effect of a suggestion is determined not only by its *force* but by its *duration* as well.

III. *Size, Form, Decoration, Color, and Illumination of Store, Comfortable Service, Waiting Chairs, Courteous Attendance, etc.*—This is a more or less indirect form of solicitation, but a very successful one, other things being approximately equal. It is an indirect appeal to the *feelings* exclusively, hence is a distinct psychological type of advertising.

IV. *Printed and Stamped Novelties, as Lead Pencils, Paper Weights, Note Books, Calendars, Knives, Rulers, Tapes, Toys, Puzzles, etc.*—The value of these depends on their *utility*, which ensures their constant observation; their *appropriateness*, which should reinforce the mere name; and their *distribution* to the right parties, those who do the buying. I have heard of a leather wallet handed out by one John Bauer, grocer, which amply fulfilled its purpose, and led its owner time after time to John Bauer's counter. I recall, also, quantities of cheap memorandum books advertising Hostetter's Bitters which always found their resting place in the street or stove. It is probable that this medium, if carefully handled, is capable of good results and in the adequate form is not sufficiently utilized.

One of the strongest points in it is the element of *good will* created by a gift. We instinctively feel approval of the man who gives us something, and the psychology of *good will* in the novelty could be developed at great length. This is the

PRINCIPLES OF APPEAL AND RESPONSE

basis of the old idea of salesmanship *à la carte,* and though the idea is being abandoned by salesmen, this is not because it was not good in its day. It needs a rest, and soon will be as effective as ever. A good discussion of the principles underlying this type of appeal may be found in Bunting's "Specialty Advertising."

V. *Registers, Directories, Theater Programs, etc.,* Resembling Class II.—Advertisements here do not hope to compete in interest with other contents of the medium. They utilize moments of monotony or other incidental moments. The advertisements, for instance, in the directory cannot hope to compete with the reason for opening the book. They are read while waiting for "central," while waiting for the curtain to rise, or for the porter to bring in the baggage. Hence publicity or reminder will be their chief aim, except in so far as they are classified advertisements: hotels, restaurants, garages, liveries, etc.

VI. *Delivery Wagons, Street Banners, Floats, etc.*—These are commonly used for emphasizing places of business, for invitation, or for mere publicity, but also can be utilized for atmospheric effect, hence resemble Class III.

VII. *Samples, Catalogues, Agents, Traveling Men.*—The firm here comes directly to the buyer.

ANALYSIS OF TASK AND MEDIA

There is little or no question of attention. The personal element of the appeal usually guarantees initial attention and also has much to do in determining the further course of the response.

VIII. In a separate class we may include the personal communication, the form letter, the "follow-up" literature of booklet and pamphlet. This form of solicitation seems to constitute a connecting link between public advertising and the direct work of agents and salesmen. There seems at present to be some uncertainty among advertising men as to whether such appeals should so far as possible simulate personal correspondence, or whether, for instance, the form letter should be frankly impersonal. This is not a point on which *a priori* opinions have much weight. Experimental tests are needed before any safe conclusions can be drawn. An "armchair psychology" could easily specify and generalize and dogmatize here, but an experimental science must wait for more data.

Having taken this general view of the situation, let us now consider the four tasks, and study the psychological factors involved in each.

CHAPTER IV

THE FIRST TASK: CATCHING THE ATTENTION

Attention may be defined in two ways: **(1)** As *an act of adjustment*—or we may speak first of the act of attention. This is what happens when we take notice of a stimulus. It is almost synonymous with perceiving, and means that the given stimulus has become clear, and that there has been an act of accommodation in the sense organ employed—eye, ear, finger tips—which tends to bring about still clearer perception.

(2) This is the point at which we plainly distinguish attention according to its second definition—as a *state of consciousness,* or the state of attention. This attentive state is characterized by the dominance of one idea, image, impression, or a set of these and the subordination of all others. Consciousness always has a focal point, and this focal point is always occupied by the thing to which we are attending at the time. We may represent this state by some such figure as a wave, the crest corresponding to the focal point

FIRST TASK: CATCHING THE ATTENTION

and the slope corresponding to the margin of the field; or we may liken it to the field of vision which always has a fixation point which is clear and a margin which is obscure. The following figures will serve as examples:

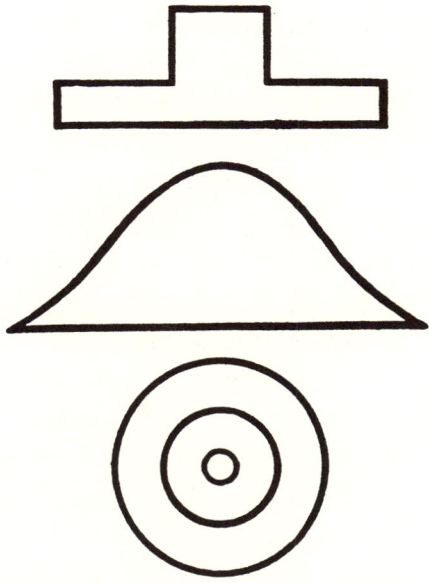

FORMS OF FOCAL POINTS OF ATTENTION

The matter of attention is not wholly an arbitrary one. The individual consciousness does not deliberately decide what shall be attended to and what not by an act of will. If it did the field of

PRINCIPLES OF APPEAL AND RESPONSE

advertising and selling would find itself astonishingly limited in its field of effective appeal.

But the act of attention is largely controlled by heredity, past experience, mood, interest, and character of the individual. Far down in the scale of animal life we can detect the rudimentary basis of what we call attention. There we call it "prepotency of stimuli." We find these lower forms indifferent and unresponsive to many forms of stimulation, but reacting vigorously and quickly to others. These "prepotent stimuli," we find, are highly important in the life of the animal concerned, although, so far as we know, he is utterly unaware of their significance. Thus, the cock-roach always retreats from the light toward the shadow, while the moth leaves darkness for light, even singeing its wings through the irresistible attraction of the flame. The young chick pecks instinctively at certain kinds of objects, the new-born kitten is attracted by certain impressions of touch and smell and reacts to them. Even among the microscopic animals tropisms are found—certain strong and apparently mechanical reactions of approach and appropriation directed toward certain colors, objects, temperatures, etc.

So in human consciousness, not all stimuli become effective. The phenomenon of *adaptation*

FIRST TASK: CATCHING THE ATTENTION

clearly shows this. We soon become adapted to the presence of the hat on our head, the clothes on our back, even to the pebble in our shoe or the temperature of the stoking room. We are constantly passing things without seeing or hearing them. We come in from the night and do not know whether or not the stars are out, whether or not the evening train just came in, whether or not we locked the door behind us. There are two reasons for this apparent obtuseness:

1. *The range of attention,* which we shall later see to be extremely limited, so that at any given moment we can attend to a very few things only, being oblivious to or only vaguely conscious of all else that is happening.
2. *Attention follows interest.*—Generally speaking, we attend to things because they interest us or have some vital import in our lives. We cannot attend to things that do not have, from one point of view or another, *interest* for us, for all that we mean by the interest which a thing has is its power to attract us, to lead us about and to direct our action toward it.

PRINCIPLES OF APPEAL AND RESPONSE

There are two kinds of interesting things:

A. The first kind includes things which are interesting only because of their consequences—their immediate or remote results—such stimuli as the creaking of an axle, a sudden flash of light, the report made by a bursting tire, palpitation of the heart. These things have no intrinsic interest; we do not care to sit and contemplate them for their own sake. But they may mean some danger, they may require some act of adjustment on our part, etc. These incentives to attention we may describe by the word *mechanical*. To such stimuli we attend only until we have learned their significance, have discovered whether or not their consequences are to be important. Then we turn at once to things which may be in themselves interesting. Only children and savages are interested in these mechanical incentives for their own sake. We shall see later that this type of incentive is well represented in current devices for advertising and selling goods.

B. In contrast with this group of mechanical incentives stands another type of appeal which is in and for itself interesting—a baseball game, a battleship, an advertising speech by the Mayor, a Hecker's food advertisement, the rainbow, a gorgeous sunset, may serve as examples. Ap-

FIRST TASK: CATCHING THE ATTENTION

peals of this sort we may designate *interest* incentives. Irrespective of any consequences, either immediate or remote, we find these things interesting, intrinsically interesting. We not only attend to them initially, but our attention is held by them through many consecutive moments or hours. And this type of appeal we shall also find represented in current appeals employed in the business of distributing goods.

CAUSES OF ATTENTION

There are four principal ways in which attention may be brought about:

- (a) By increased relative intensity of the stimulus.
- (b) By the intrinsic interest of the stimulus.
- (c) By accommodation of the sense organs to be used, so that the incoming impression may be received to best advantage.
- (d) By preperception—anticipatory preparation, from within, of the ideational centers to be employed when the stimulus arrives.

Attention is often classified as voluntary, involuntary, and spontaneous. These forms are

PRINCIPLES OF APPEAL AND RESPONSE

clearly seen to represent only different combinations of the four methods just enumerated. Thus voluntary attention is brought about by methods (c) and (d). Involuntary attention is that produced by method (a), and spontaneous attention that effected by methods (a) and (b). It is apparent that advertising can employ only two of the four possible methods of attracting attention, namely those two methods by which spontaneous attention is brought about. It follows, then, that these two methods must be used as effectively as possible. It is, of course, further true that when we come to the second task, that of holding attention, we shall see that voluntary attention may also come to play an important part.

RESULTS AND LAWS OF ATTENTION

Before further analyzing these methods of intensity and interest, let us learn what the result of attention will be when we have once secured it. The results of attention will determine to a great degree the nature of our next inquiry: "How can an appeal attract attention?" Before we turn to advertisements in particular, what are the results or laws of attention, in general?

I. *The process attended to becomes clearer and more distinct than others.* This is well illustrated

FIRST TASK: CATCHING THE ATTENTION

by attention to the hidden figure in a puzzle-picture. Attend to the figure, it looms up clearly, while the rest of the picture fades into the obscure margin of consciousness. Attend to the background, on the other hand, and this in turn becomes sharply defined, while the hidden figure is blurred.

II. *The process attended to becomes more intense,* especially if it was originally very faint. Attend to a very faint light or a sound—a star or the tick of a watch—or attend to a particular instrument in an orchestra. The stimulus attended to becomes not only clearer but it seems to be louder as well.

III. *The process attended to becomes increased in duration,* especially when it is otherwise very short. Moments of time, if attended to, pass slowly. The long drawn out diminuendo of a violin may seem continued after the actual vibration has ceased, especially if the suggestion is reinforced by continued movement of the bow. The headlines which compel strong attention or the cuts that attract the eye persist in consciousness according to the degree of attention bestowed upon them. Because they persist longer they have greater opportunity for association with other experiences, and hence are more likely to be recalled than some other processes attended to less intently. This result is closely related to the next law.

IV. *The process attended to rises more quickly into consciousness* than do other processes entering simultaneously. We can illustrate this by the "complication experiment" of the laboratory. If in this experiment a sound and flash of light are so arranged as to occur at the same moment, they will seem not synchronous but successive, the one attended to appearing to precede the other. Under this law we may also put the general fact that at a subsequent time, if there is occasion to recall the process, the one attended to most strongly tends to recur more quickly and easily than others.

The foregoing related laws are both theoretically and practically important. From them it follows not only that an appeal should be able to attract attention, but that, other things being equal, it should attract as much attention as possible. For the appeal compelling the strongest degree of attention will be clearer, more intense, and more active than that less strongly attended to. As we shall see later, the power of a suggestion depends not only on the fact of attention but also on the degree of attention.

FIRST TASK: CATCHING THE ATTENTION

V. *Attention is the basis of every will-act,* and the only basis. Every idea or impression has its inevitable motor issue. Nervous energy, once generated, must be liberated, discharged, over an outgoing pathway. Just what pathway is taken is immaterial so far as the nervous system is concerned. It follows, then, that the response to the stimulus which is strongly attended to drains off the energy generated by marginal stimuli, with the result that this response is strengthened. This is the basis of an act of will or choice. It is the fundamental principle of response. When two processes divide the field of attention between them, each tends to set off its appropriate response. The result is two weak responses, or, if the two stimuli are antagonistic, no response at all. If my attention now shifts from one to the other, I vacillate, am weak-willed, undecided. But the moment that I attend exclusively to either idea, its motor consequences ensue at once, and I have responded to the suggestion. I have willed. This is the fundamental law of suggestion and response. Every idea, if attended to exclusively, tends to realize itself in action. We will have this principle before us again when we come to the third task of the appeal.

Do not be impatient with this prolonged analysis of the attentive state. We are trying to get at the very bottom of the principles of appeal and response, and this rather abstract examination is essential to the more concrete things that are soon to follow. To discuss many other extremely interesting results would be to go too far afield for the purposes of this book. But there are two more principles that must not be omitted. From the practical point of view they are the most important of the seven. They cover not so much the results of attention as they do the behavior of attention itself.

VI. *This law is that attention fluctuates,* comes in beats or pulses; the state of attention is of short duration. Our consciousness cannot remain intent on one object or idea. It must roam about, much like a bird flying from bough to bough. It cannot remain on the same bough constantly. It must, after a given time, leap over to another bough and then return, or else it must shift its position on the same bough every so often, changing from one foot to another or facing about or lighting on various parts of the same perch.

The length of these waves or pulses of attention is usually about four seconds in our experimental researches, two seconds coming to the crest and two seconds dying away. Much work is be-

FIRST TASK: CATCHING THE ATTENTION

ing done by modern experimentalists to discover the neurological reason for this rhythm of attention. It constitutes a fascinating field of modern investigation. But, here again, to go farther would be to digress.

I show you here the record of such a laboratory experiment, taken by one of my students.

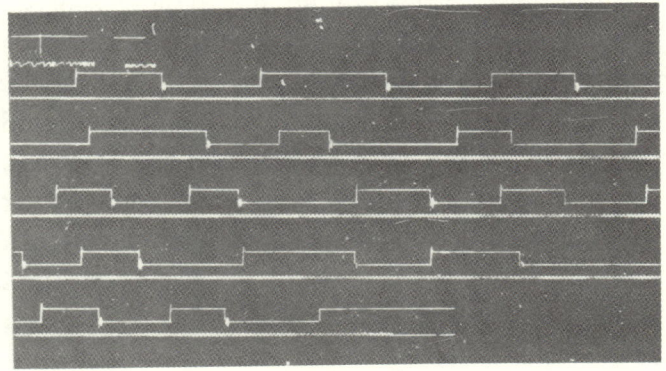

AN EXPERIMENT ON ATTENTION. The wavy line marks off fifths of seconds. When the straight line is on the low level, a faint visual stimulus was in the field of attention. The high level indicates the disappearance of the stimulus from attention.

This law of attention will be our chief concern when we come to the second talk, that of Holding Attention.

VII. Finally, in this abstract analysis, we must include the general law that *the range of attention is limited.* We may distinguish here between

PRINCIPLES OF APPEAL AND RESPONSE

the *focus* of attention, and the *margin* of attention. You will all remember in this connection that five acts have long been recognized as the artistic limit for a drama, five feet for a line, and preferably five lines for a stanza, five chief characters in a dialogue. And these are all cases where one has the sympathy of the reader from the beginning. In framing the artistic solicitation for his eye, it is better to be on the safe side and allow, say, one fact to the focus, one to the field, and one to the margin. But it may be said here that it is five *units* that can be compassed in a single act of attention. If I expose five or six small dots for a fraction of a second you can report their number correctly, but more than that many you cannot perceive accurately. You can, however, see five letters, each composed of dots, just as easily, and even five words, if the words are familiar enough to be perceived as units.

These facts have a very practical bearing. They mean that the ideal headline should not contain over five units. Usually these units will be single words. But as a matter of fact a sentence can be grasped as a whole providing it can be broken into, say, four phrase units of perhaps four words each, or, preferably, three. If I say, "The proper length for a comfortable sentence is felt to be

FIRST TASK: CATCHING THE ATTENTION

about sixteen words," my sentence is seen to be thus constructed. It has four phrase elements of three or four words each, and the sentence is easily grasped as a whole. But if I say, "By a careful experimentally conducted investigation of the laws of attention, psychologists have been led to conclude that the most favorable sentence length for the average reader is, under ordinary conditions, approximately sixteen single words," you are dismayed by the length and structure of the sentence. It falls to pieces, requiring more than one effort of attention. We may say, then, that nine to sixteen words make a clear and easily read sentence. That is, of course, only an approximation. The actual number in any given case will depend on the ease with which the single words group themselves into phrase units. But good headlines will seldom be found with more than nine and usually not more than five words. We shall have a great deal to say about this law of attention when we come to consider the second task.

CHAPTER V

MECHANICAL INCENTIVES

So much for the state of attention itself. Let us now turn to the concrete ways of bringing it about. You will recall that the advertisement can only work through spontaneous attention, and that this state can be brought about by two means: (1) By the *relative intensification* of the stimuli. Under this head comes the group of methods which we have designated *mechanical devices*. (2) By the *intrinsic interest* of the stimulus. This group we classify as *interest incentives*. Naturally and inevitably, through the very structure of our nervous systems, we attend to stimuli of these two kinds. The basis for their power over us lies either in the physiology of all nerve tissue, in the inherited results of remote ancestral experience, or in our own peculiar past history and desires for the future.

Of the two groups, the mechanical devices, although the chief means employed by past and even by most contemporary advertising, are the least

MECHANICAL INCENTIVES

potent and in many cases are futile, so far as real returns are concerned. I have often been asked to state what in my opinion would be the next advance step in advertising. I should say that the most effective change for the better that could be made is the change from mechanical devices to interest incentives. But the mechanical devices are much used at present, and will probably always be employed to a greater or less degree; and for certain types of advertising mechanical devices are effective. The mechanical devices fall into six chief classes according as the method used is a variation of *intensity, magnitude, motion, contrast, surrounding* or *position.*

1. INTENSITY

Other things being equal, we will, of course, attend to the strongest stimulus. We listen to the shrillest newsboy, the loudest barker at the side show, just as we let the thunder distract us from the chirping of crickets. But this is not due to genuine interest in the strong stimulus. A strong stimulus causes nervous shock and is likely to constitute or indicate a source of danger to the organism. Those of our ancestors who failed to notice intense stimuli perished in avalanches, tornadoes, etc. Only those survived

PRINCIPLES OF APPEAL AND RESPONSE

whose nervous systems were sensitive to abrupt changes, and they passed their constitution on down to us. Besides, a strong stimulus means much physical energy impinging on our sense organs, and this sets up strong nervous currents which force their way inward in spite of our wishes. Fortunately, however, advertising has but little use for this device. Advertising is chiefly a visual matter, still more chiefly a matter of printing, and the range of possible intensities in printing is very slight. The intense lights of an electric sign, the brilliant colors of a billboard placard may force us to look in their direction. But they may force us just as quickly to look away again. They may attract attention, but they lack the power to hold it. All advertising that depends for its success on the mere noise it makes, on the sheer intensity of its horn, is likely to find the two to be in inverse ratio. Only savages and children, as we have said, delight in intensity of stimulus for its own sake. Savages beat their tom-toms and children pound and kick from delight in the activity of a sense organ, and perhaps also because their undeveloped senses do not get the same degree of sensation from the intense stimulation that we do.

The rumble of the elevated train never attracts

MECHANICAL INCENTIVES

my attention unless it interferes with my present activity, and even then it does not attract but repels me. But the plaintive squeal of some old woman's hand organ, the whistle of a fraternity brother, some curious brogue in the speech of a passerby, some comic incident of the street, attracts me at once in spite of its mildness. A man slipped on the icy walk the other day. He made no noise, but slipped down softly and flatly. The negro garbage collector who happened to be passing saw him just as he was clambering to his feet again. "Do it again," shouted the driver of the garbage wagon, "I didn't see you that time." This trivial incident had greater attention value with the driver than did the roar of the traffic around him.

The noisy honk of the automobile does not attract you but gets you out of the way. The intense stimulus means danger. The soft siren call on the automobile had to be abandoned, not because people would not attend to it, but because they did not run away from it. If you want to appeal to children and to savages, then, you may use the intensity device with some degree of effectiveness. For civilized people and grown-ups the blaring seldom attracts attention beyond itself.

PRINCIPLES OF APPEAL AND RESPONSE

2. MAGNITUDE

Much has been written concerning the relative attention value of small and large spaces, cards, signs, cuts, type, etc., in advertising, and several suggestive attempts have been made to study the matter experimentally. The opinion of advertising men seems to point to proportionate increase in values with the amount of space used. The use of full-page advertisements has increased, as Scott has shown. Thus in 1892 the *Century Magazine* contained only 18 **per** cent. full-page advertisements as compared with 43 per cent. in 1908. There is also a tendency to use two page "spreads" more and more.

Scott tested over 500 people, giving each the same magazine (*Century*), asking them to "look it over" in a general way, but not to read long articles or poetry. After having examined the magazine for 10 minutes, each was asked to write out all he remembered of all the advertisements he had seen. The same investigator also made up a magazine by choosing 100 pages of varied advertising pages from a large number of magazines, so as to get variety of material, size, form, type, etc. These pages were then bound together along with reading matter and 60 adults

MECHANICAL INCENTIVES

were asked to "look through" the magazine, for an average time of 10 minutes. Each then mentioned each advertisement remembered, gave its contents, and was then again given the magazine and asked to indicate all the pages now recognized as having been seen before.

The results of these experiments were as follows: In the number of times the advertisement was mentioned from memory, in the number of times it was later recognized, and in the number of times it conveyed definite information as to the general class of goods advertised, the specific name or brand of the goods, name and address of the firm, price, etc., the rule was general that the full page was more than twice as effective as the one-half page. The half-page was also more than twice as effective as the quarter-page, and this in turn more than twice as effective as the eighth-page. Scott's general conclusion is: "The attention and memory value of an advertisement increases as the size of the advertisement increases, and the increase of value is greater than the increase in the amount of space used."

But Scott points out the fact that the *quality* of the advertisement, that is its content, is even more important than its size. Indeed, it is quite probable that the increase in value with increase in space, in these experiments, was chiefly due to difference in the contents of the space. A large advertisement is likely to be different from a small one in things other than mere magnitude. The large space permits the use of pictures, of suggested action, removes competition by monopolizing space, and also makes possible greater contrast and clearness. It is probable, then, that the increased value of a large space in these experiments came not from the mere fact of magnitude, but from the presence of *interest* incentives which the magnitude makes possible, but of course does not necessarily involve.

When the content of the space is kept constant in character and interest there is no evidence that the increase in returns is nearly so great as the increase in space and cost. Of course, the larger advertisement will be more likely to be seen, but it must be seen and read twice as much or more than this to justify the increase in cost, if a whole page is compared with a half page. Time after time the results of mail order advertising are said to have shown only an increased cost per reply when greater space was employed. The writer has on hand sets of advertisements in which the character of the content, the medium, and the commodity advertised have all been kept constant and

MECHANICAL INCENTIVES

the returns measured by the number of inquiries for booklets, etc. The results from these sets suggest a more or less definite law of increase under such circumstances, namely: *the number of inquiries tends to increase as the square root of the amount of space used.* That is to say, use four times the space and you double the returns; use nine times the space and you treble the returns, while to quadruple the number of replies would require sixteen times the amount of space, other factors remaining constant. Some such law of increase may, in fact, be supposed to operate in the case of all the mechanical incentives.

This is an interesting point, psychologically, for it falls in line with what is known in the laboratory as the psycho-physical law, according to which the sensation produced by a stimulus does not increase in the same ratio as does the increase in the objective intensity of the stimulus, but much more slowly, approximately as the square root of this intensity. We know that, in many other fields beyond a certain point this law of "diminishing returns" holds—to double the amount of coal consumed does not double the speed of a boat; nor can twelve laborers produce, from a given limited area of land or a given factory equipment and floor space, twice the produc-

PRINCIPLES OF APPEAL AND RESPONSE

tion of six laborers working under the same conditions.

The following series of Graphite advertisements indicates a similar law. These appeals ap-

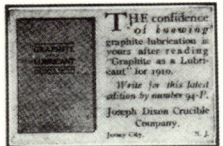

AD. NO. 1—32 REPLIES. ⅛ PAGE

peared under the same conditions of commodity and medium, and all three rely on the same general type of attention device. No. 1, an advertisement occupying one-eighth of a page, brought

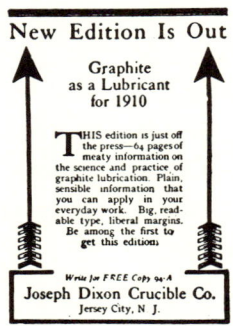

AD. NO. 2—32 REPLIES. ¼ PAGE

32 replies. Several others of the same size and type brought from 21 to 42 replies. No. 2 presents the same appeal, with perhaps a somewhat

MECHANICAL INCENTIVES

better layout, so far as initial attention value is concerned, and it occupied one-quarter page, twice the amount of space occupied by No. 1. But it

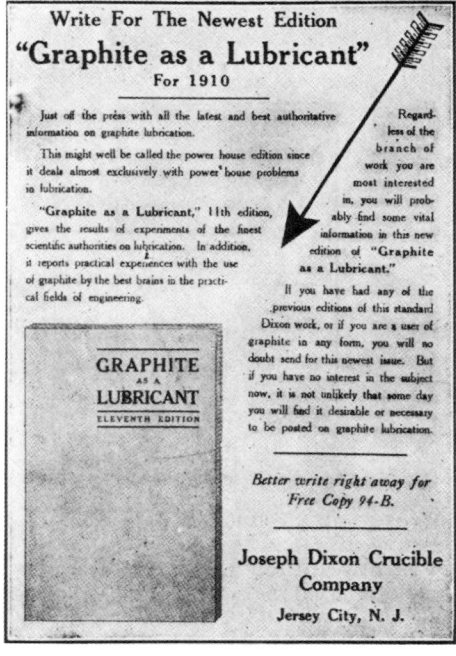

AD. NO. 3—75 REPLIES. FULL PAGE

brought only the same number of replies. No. 3, very similar to both 1 and 2 in general content, but occupying a full page, brought only 75 replies. That is to say, it is four times the size of

PRINCIPLES OF APPEAL AND RESPONSE

No. 1, but brought only twice as many replies, as we should expect, under the square root law.

Of course if the style of the appeal is changed, these results will vary correspondingly. Thus No. 4, which introduces an *interest* incentive (picture, suggested activity) is no larger than No. 2, but

AD. NO. 4—186 REPLIES. ¼ PAGE

brought 186 replies. This last appeal will be referred to again under the section on suggested activity.

Münsterberg has recently reported experiments designed to measure the value of large spaces, appearing once, as compared with that of smaller spaces appearing often enough to make the final space occupied equal in both cases. Based on the total attention and memory values, the relative values are as follows:

MECHANICAL INCENTIVES

Full page, appearing once	.33
Half page, appearing twice	.30
Quarter page, appearing four times	.49
Eighth page, eight times	.44
Twelfth page, twelve times	.47

On the basis of the chances of the advertisement being included among the first 10 remembered, in time, the values are:

Full page, appearing once	0.5
Half page, appearing twice	1.2
Quarter page, four times	2.9
Eighth page, eight times	2.3
Twelfth page, twelve times	2.4

In general, that is to say, the small spaces repeated are more effective than the large space appearing but once. Of course, these values are not entirely dependent on the difference in space, but also upon the factor of *repetition,* which is in itself a form of mechanical device, if the appeal is attended to when repeated.

Further information bearing in this same general direction is afforded by several experiments conducted by Dr. E. K. Strong, Jr., Research Fellow in Columbia University, for the New York Advertising Men's League and the National Association of Advertising Managers. Perhaps the only argument in favor of magnitude is that advanced by some practical advertising men, to the effect that the additional prestige and suggestion

PRINCIPLES OF APPEAL AND RESPONSE

of prosperity conveyed by the large space employed tend to create a favorable impression in the mind of the reader.

So far as the experience of the psychologist goes, mere magnitude possesses the same defect as does mere intensity, and to even greater degree. The large object does attract initial attention. Unusually large things possess a certain importance in the life of any animal; they are likely to be dangerous, unmanageable, to be avoided, etc. Therefore, the first appearance of a mammoth billboard or electric sign will attract attention. But as soon as the real character, the harmlessness, of the thing is learned, it will be passed by unnoticed, just as are the Singer building, the Metropolitan tower, the *Imperator,* and the enormous signs and displays of the Great White Way. Magnitude in advertising is probably of real value only in so far as it makes possible certain more genuine interest appeals.

The question of size of type has also received frequent discussion and investigation. Gale found progressive increase in attention value with increase in size of type from two to six millimeters. He gives the table on page 73:

Scott studied two kinds of type with the same body, but one of which had light and the other

MECHANICAL INCENTIVES

heavy face. What he tried to discover was the time required to read these two kinds of type and the number of errors made in such reading. For the light faced type the total time of six observers was 147 minutes, the number of errors 132. For the heavy face, the total time was 129 minutes, the

TABLE IV

Height Type	Relative Legibility, Per Cent.		
	Men	Women	Average
2 mm	8.7	11.6	10.1
4 mm	20.2	15.8	18.0
5 mm	27.7	27.5	27.6
6 mm	43.0	45.0	44.0

errors 91. Such legibility tests should be carried further. But it must not be supposed that legibility and attention value are the same thing. It is in general true that the more easily type can be read the more agreeably will the people read it. But they will not be likely to read it just because it is legible. Under a given set of conditions a certain type size, a certain spacing and massing will be most favorable. But adequate tests of this matter, from the practical point of view, have not been made. More will be said on this topic in another connection.

The writer would, then, be inclined to stress the

futility of mere size as an effective advertising device. On psychological grounds the small advertisement with *intrinsic interest* of some sort or other—color, cut, action suggested, comic, appeal to special instinct or feeling or value, will be more effective, and less expensive as well.

3. MOTION

The third mechanical incentive to attention is that of a moving stimulus. An object in motion has much higher attention value than a stationary thing. This is true far down in the animal scale. One may approach very close to a wild animal so long as one's accessory movements are inhibited. A squirrel may perch on my hand, but the slightest movement of a near-by object suffices to send him scurrying. Hold your finger, for instance, in the edge of your field of vision; you are not able to see it, but wriggle it a little and its image becomes at once distinct. Psychologically there are two reasons why this should be true. One is an interest reason, viz., the fact that moving objects are more likely to contain in them possibilities of good or evil. Hence from earliest experience moving objects have become of unusual interest and significance for us. The second reason is a mechanical one, viz., that sensation is

MECHANICAL INCENTIVES

only consciousness of change. We become rapidly adapted to a constant stimulus so that we fail to notice the weight of our hats, the temperature of the room we are in, the odors of the subway. But the moment a change occurs it is detected, because it involves fresh and unfatigued sensitive surface. So keen is our sense of movement that we can detect the motion of a point on the skin long before we can tell the direction in which it is traveling. This is the basis for the high attention value of rotating barber signs and display shelves, shifting bulletin boards, moving pictures, flash lights, moving frames in shoe and hat stores. The Old Dutch Cleanser in Harlem, and the Heatherbloom petticoat sign are instances of the initial value of movement, as are running lights and serpentines. The use of movement is certainly one of the most effective of the mechanical incentives, but it has in common with all mechanical devices the fault of failing to hold attention when once it is caught, and the further defect of rapidly undergoing adaptation. You must not confuse the actual use of movement with the somewhat related principle of suggested action. Nothing has higher attention value than the reproduction of a fellow creature in action. But this is much different from the crude use of mere motion of an inanimate object. It is strictly an interest incentive and will be considered fully under that heading.

4. CONTRAST

The next important mechanical device is that of *contrast*. Because sensation is the consciousness of change, any great or striking difference in the intensity, size, color or character of the stimulus produces an unusually vivid consciousness. The gradual appearance of an electric sign would pass unnoticed, but the alternation of its sudden illumination and disappearance at once attracts the attention. In the same way a striking difference between foreground and background has strong attention value, and black on white, blue on yellow, red on green are the most striking combinations of color, because the two members of each pair are contrasting in color. A small man and a large woman, a Shetland pony harnessed alongside a draught horse, would have a similar attention value. So, in looking through the advertisements of a magazine, any sharp departure from the usual appearance of the pages in size, form, color, style of type, content, size of type, kind of cut, possesses strong attention value. And in our day of manifold advertisement pages this is an important item. The defect of the contrast incentive again is that of all the mechanical devices. To be effective it must be reinforced by an interest incentive, or else it fails to hold the attention it has gained by sheer force.

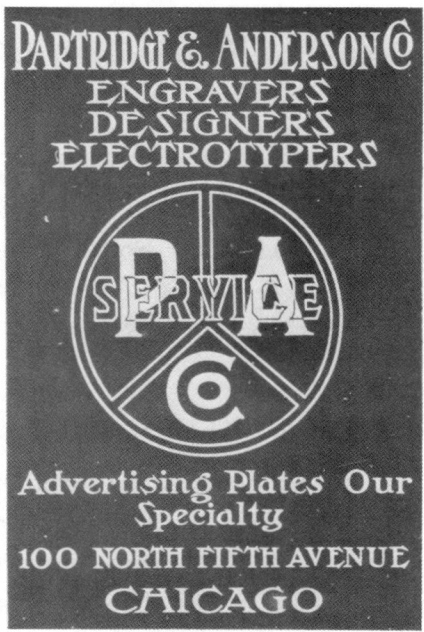

WHITE ON BLACK

The writer has frequently been asked why black on white attracts more attention than white on black. The contrast is apparently the same here, and the principle of irradiation would lead us to expect just the opposite result. The reason is probably that we habitually associate *dark spaces* with objects and *light spaces* with background—with air, opening, sky, water, etc. It is always the positive, active features of our environment, the *objects,* to which we give special notice. Backgrounds have no particular importance except as they set off objects. So when black letters are seen on white the letters attract attention. But when white letters appear on black, they seem to be merely *holes* in the *object,* which is now the dark part. Hence we do not attend to the form, etc., of the letters. So far as acuity and legibility go there is no difference between the two arrangements.

5. ISOLATION

Closely allied to contrast is another factor —the *absence of counter attraction*. Consciousness is never empty. If it were it would not be consciousness. This means that we *must* attend to *something,* and, for the most part, to something in the outside world. In the absence of counter attraction consciousness fixates the one thing in the field. The value of monopolizing the whole space, of eliminating competing appeals by employing plenty of white space, etc., has its basis

MECHANICAL INCENTIVES

here. Little more need be said. The difficulties with this device are: (1) that we quickly become adapted to its artificial character, (2) that there

ATTENTION VALUE OF ISOLATION

is always more than one field open to consciousness, and it is necessary to make the page, wall, side of the street, etc., have some *intrinsic* interest before the absence of counter attraction in that particular field has a chance to work.

PRINCIPLES OF APPEAL AND RESPONSE

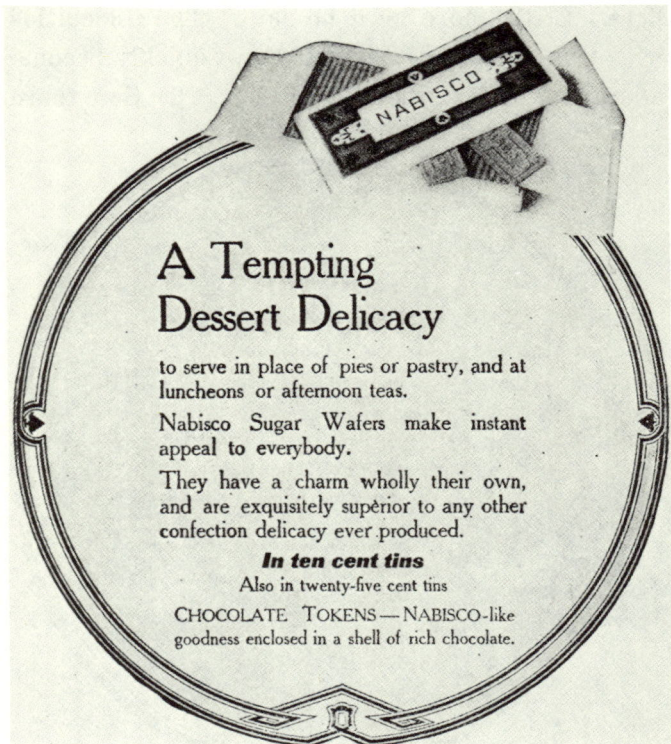

ABSENCE OF COUNTER ATTRACTION

6. POSITION

The final mechanical device is that of *position*. Because of certain habitual fixation tendencies of the eyes in reading and observing, certain positions on a printed page, a bulletin board, etc., have greater attention value than others. Thus, in

Gale's experiments the left side of the page was found to have greater attention value than the right. This result would follow from the tendency to begin on the left and read to the right, so that in a quick exposure such as Gale gave the left side would have the advantage, and especially so since he studied the page when it was taken out of the magazine and presented as a flat surface. Starch experimented with nonsense syllables placed in different positions in a pamphlet of twelve pages. On the third and eighth pages the same syllable occurred. Fifty people looked through the pamphlet and then wrote out all the syllables remembered. Of those occurring on the left side of the page 44 per cent. were recalled, while 56 per cent. of those on the right were recalled. This contradicts Gale's results.

The experiments are complicated by the fact that in reading the eye has a second tendency to fixate the object in each hand—the part of the page held at normal reading distance. This will be in magazines, and especially in newspapers, the two outside columns, one of which is on the right, the other on the left. Starch's experiments further erred in using such unusual and artificial things as nonsense syllables which vary greatly among themselves in attention and memory

PRINCIPLES OF APPEAL AND RESPONSE

value. From general knowledge of the laws of reading and eye movement, however, I will venture to prophesy that in flat surfaces the left side will be found to be most favorable, in newspaper pages the *outside* spaces, that is, the left on the left-hand pages and the right on the right-hand pages, while on magazine pages there will be little difference found.

A second question relating to position concerns the relative value of the top and bottom of the page. Psychologically there are two factors that work here:

(1) We tend to find *meaning* in the top of things, the faces of our fellow men, the branches of trees, etc. We begin to read at the top of the page. Further, in reading, experiments show that the upper part of the printed letters is more significant than the lower part and that the eye does not run along the middle of a printed or written line but rather along a line between the middle of the small letters and the tops of the high ones, that is, a line somewhat above the center.

(2) In fixating a general object, especially a work of art, a picture, wall, etc., there is a constant tendency to fixate the center. This gives us

the best view of the object as a whole and also enables us to perceive its unitary structure, balance, proportion, etc.

Here are, then, two tendencies. The result is a compromise, in which the space between top and center has greatest advantage. Experiment confirms this result. Thus, in Starch's tests, the value of the upper half of pages was 61 per cent., as against 39 per cent. for the lower half, when the page was divided into quarters. When it was divided only into halves the same law held, the values being, upper half 54 per cent., lower half 46 per cent. Gale, studying flat surfaces, divided into horizontal quarters, found that the quarter just above the middle was strongest, and the bottom weakest.

Finally, in this problem of position there is the question of preferred pages. The fact of preferred pages is recognized by magazine rates, but the policies here are quite discordant, some making great and some relatively small extra charge for preferred positions. Starch studied this problem using nonsense syllables with his twelve-page pamphlet. He found the following results:

DATA
Total number recalled	261
Average number on outside cover recalled	34
Average number on inside cover recalled	26
Average number on other pages recalled	17

PRINCIPLES OF APPEAL AND RESPONSE

This indicates the outer cover to be twice as effective, and the inside cover to be half again as effective as the ordinary inside pages.

Using real advertisements instead of the syllables, the results were: preferred positions, average 19.2 times; non-preferred positions, average 6.5 times. But these figures are highly unreliable because the advertisements themselves differ greatly in attention value, familiarity and interest. Furthermore, all the inside pages are lumped together, with no attempt to discriminate between, say, page 3 and page 7, or between back half and front half of the pamphlet. Moreover, the value of other preferred pages, such as those next to the reading matter, is not considered.

The following figures resulted from a preliminary experiment performed by one of my students. A magazine containing 10 pages of advertising matter in the front section and 10 in the back section was chosen. A set of trade marks (geometrical forms of solid black and of approximately the same area) was affixed, one to the center of each of these pages. The relative attention value of each of these forms, when all were seen under the same conditions, was determined by a careful experiment with 25 people. After this had been done it was possible to allow for the dif-

MECHANICAL INCENTIVES

ferences in attention value, due not to the page itself, but to the form which it happened to carry. Thus, if the form on page 3 was found to have 2.5 times the attention value of the form on page 7, the results from page 7, when multiplied by 2.5, might be supposed to be absolutely comparable with the results from page 3, and any difference between the two, after this compensation had been made, would reflect nothing but the relative attention value of the two pages themselves. The experiment thus attempted to conform to the first requirement of a scientific experiment (curiously neglected in reported tests of advertising values), namely, that the only variable factor be that which is being specifically investigated, or that, if other factors vary, this variation be also measured and reckoned with in the valuation of the final returns. The set of trade marks, with their relative attention value, will appear in another connection.

A group of 25 subjects was then allowed to look through the magazine for a limited time, without being told the purpose of the experiment. Each subject took the magazine from a shelf of books, and looked through it in his own way. He was later presented with a complete set of 50 geometrical forms and requested to pick out the

PRINCIPLES OF APPEAL AND RESPONSE

20 forms that he had previously seen in the magazine.

The results were then transformed into comparable quantities, in the manner just described, and in this way the relative attention value of the various pages, when the magazine was handled in this way, was determined. The following table resulted:

TABLE V

Front Section	Value in Per Cent.	Back Section	Value in Per Cent.
Page		Page	
1...............	34.4	11...............	48.6
2 or 3..........	44.2	12 or 13........	21.5
4 or 5..........	38.0	14 or 15........	31.5
6 or 7..........	43.9	16 or 17........	30.4
8 or 9..........	39.1	18 or 19........	32.4
10..............	69.0	20..............	20.0

Average of front section, 43.4; average of back section, 30.0.

Several facts are clearly evident here:

1. The value of the front section is almost 50 per cent. better than that of the back section.
2. The best page of all is the page next to the reading matter in front (page 10, 69 per cent.). The next best is the page next to the reading matter behind (page 11, 48.6 per cent.).

MECHANICAL INCENTIVES

3. The front cover (page 1) and the back cover (page 20) turn out to be the poorest pages of the whole twenty.
4. Aside from the front cover and the page next the reading matter, all the front pages are of about equal value, when the section is limited to 10 pages.
5. Aside from the back cover and the page next to the reading matter, all the back pages are of about equal value.

Here are a number of experimental facts that are in striking contrast with the common theories of preferred position. To be sure, the results cannot, without further verification, be transferred to conditions other than those in which the experiment was performed. But other tests seem to indicate that all the rules which hold in this experiment also hold when the sections are much larger, when actual advertisements are considered instead of geometrical forms, and when the magazine is taken home and read in the ordinary way.

The following curves give the results of an elaborate experiment performed by Dr. Strong, for the purpose of determining the relative value of preferred pages in a larger magazine than the

PRINCIPLES OF APPEAL AND RESPONSE

small one employed in the case of the experiments I have just described. This experiment conformed even more closely to the conditions of actual reading habits. The procedure is described

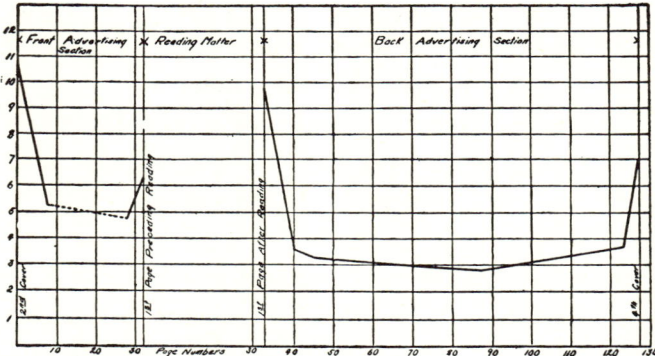

RESULTS OF ONE OF DR. STRONG'S TESTS ON ATTENTION VALUE OF DIFFERENT ADVERTISING PAGES IN EVERYBODY'S MAGAZINE. The figures at the left represent the percentage of 137 women who noticed the advertisement in the various pages. The figures across the bottom indicate the number of the page in the advertising sections. The advertisements on the covers were not considered. For example, the advertisement on the page opposite the second cover was noticed by 10½% of the women tested, the advertisement on the page just preceding reading matter by 6¼% of the women, the advertisement on the page just after reading matter by 9¾% of the women, and the advertisement on the last page opposite the third cover by 7% of the women. Contrasted with these preferred pages we find but 2¾% of the women noticing advertisements in the neighborhood of page 88—the center of the back advertising section.

by Strong as follows: "A professor assigned his class as necessary reading an article in the September issue of *Everybody's Magazine*. Each member of the class was supplied with a copy of

MECHANICAL INCENTIVES

the magazine, and was allowed to keep it one week, after which time it was to be returned to the class room. Each person was then given an envelope containing all the full-page advertisements that had appeared in the issue and a good number of others from another issue. They were requested to look through these and select those they remembered as having been in the magazine. One hundred and thirty-seven people were thus tested, ranging in age from 18 to 50. A number were married, and all were in the Domestic Science Department of Teachers College, and especially interested in problems of the household. Many are right now the buyers for homes, and most of the remainder are qualifying to become so in the near future." These results are seen to confirm all the generalizations based on the earlier experiment, except that, because of the length of time which the magazine was used, the cover pages came to have higher value than was accorded them in the earlier tests.

This completes our study of the *mechanical incentives,* their characteristics, laws, and relative values. In general we may say that these incentives are crude and unsatisfactory. After having discussed the *interest incentives* in a similar way, I shall give an account of an interesting demonstration and proof of the inferior value of the mechanical group. The essential thing about a successful appeal is that it shall be able to sustain the attention it has once caught, and the mechanical incentives in themselves fail to do this. Only attention based on interest is likely to be held long enough for the suggested idea to realize itself in action. The *interest incentives,* then, are the effective ones. A study of these factors we are to take up in the next chapter.

CHAPTER VI

INTEREST INCENTIVES

Interest incentives fall under the headings of eight chief principles. These are the most effective devices for catching the attention in a permanent way. Their chief strength is derived from the fact that the *feeling of interest,* which is essential to *sustained attention,* is the very basis of their initial attraction value. These eight incentives are the appeal through:

1. Novelty: bizarre effects, unusual devices and statements.
2. Color: brightness, tone and harmony.
3. Illustration: cuts, photographs, sketches.
4. Action: suggested activity on the part of persons or things.
5. The comic: pictorial and verbal humor.
6. Feeling tone: pleasantness, excitement, strain and their opposites.
7. Instinctive response: any appeal to a fundamental instinct.

PRINCIPLES OF APPEAL AND RESPONSE

8. Effective conceptions: appeal to established habits and ideals.

1. NOVELTY

The basis of the value of novelty as an incentive is twofold. Recall the extreme importance, in the lives of our ancestors and in our own experience, of unusual objects, new situations, unaccustomed stimuli. The organism is perfectly adapted to familiar objects, but strange ones can only set up disturbed or random responses, and hence cause the feeling of shock. We are startled by the novel. It is full of interest to us both on account of the *danger* it may contain and on account of the *good* it may afford. Hence we always attend to it closely when we discover it. This incentive is closely related to the *instinct of curiosity*. Curiosity is merely the name for our interest in the unknown or unfamiliar. Throw a strange object into the field and the horses and cattle will circle around it, sniffing, poking and snorting until they seem to have discovered all the possible sources of activity to be anticipated from the object. If the object shows no new traits, but behaves just as the old familiar objects in the pasture, the cattle soon scatter away

INTEREST INCENTIVES

and are hereafter unconcerned about it. But if it shows any new or unwonted characteristics, the

NOVELTY AS AN EFFECTIVE ATTENTION DEVICE. This also illustrates an important principle of PERCEPTION, viz., that one "sees" not so much what the sense organ affords but rather what the present stimulus has been *learned to mean*. Sensation is supplemented by perception. In the above picture only parts of the objects are given in sensation, but the objects are nevertheless perceived as wholes.

animals are interested in it for days and may be observed constantly examining it. The same is true of a child with a new toy.

Herein lies the strong attention value of all devices designed to arouse curiosity—bizarre figures, cuts, shapes, grotesque faces, novel forms and arrangements, new type faces, curious spell-

PRINCIPLES OF APPEAL AND RESPONSE

ing, unusual location or positions, catchy names, trade marks, unfamiliar media, such as kites, skyrockets, balloons, curious street walkers, window exhibitions, prize packages, lotteries, prizes, puzzles, contests, continued stories, etc. Churches

In our $35. overcoat every penny is a wise investment.

Every dollar of the $35. will work for your benefit.

If you're tired of conventional styles and colors come and see these quaint patterns and tones--shape and cut equally new.

For the conservative customer--everything dignified.

Prices from $15 to $40.

New Neckwear to harmonize with the color of the overcoat.

Of the three leading New York and London overcoats for the Fall this cut gives a general idea-- to get the exact idea come in and try 'em on.

Certainly some of these coats are extreme--very ultra radical-- plus, and let it go at that.

They are only for those who appreciate the very newest fashion.

For the man of quiet taste everything in correct conservative lines.

Overcoats $-- to $--
Suits $-- to $--

Our New York Resident Buyer sent in a few new and odd Persian designs in neckwear.

THE CONVENTIONAL

have frequently carried on advertising campaigns based on the novelty incentive, introducing unheard-of specialties and stunts into the service. Newspapers, politicians, purveyors of foodstuffs, publishers, clothiers, dealers in every commodity except perhaps large staple products, machinery,

INTEREST INCENTIVES

etc., use this incentive to advantage. The element of novelty attracts the attention initially, and, if the thing is sufficiently curious, the observer is likely to keep his attention fixed until the advertisement has been thoroughly digested.

EXTREMES MEET.
"It's only an extreme type of people who carry a fashion to its extreme limit."

This winter we've carried out the ideas expressed by the "Clothier and Furnisher"

"Dignified clothing cut on conservative lines will be the selection in demand for winter."

Our suits and overcoats while embodying all the novel features in cut and fabric are in the common-sense, becoming, fashionable class.

Suits $15 to $40.
Overcoats $15. to $45.

It's time to turn those negligee shirts out to grass.

October is the time for the stiff bosom shirt to be firm in its demands on your attention. We have 'em in short bosoms, so now all the old discomforts are avoided. Try 'em.

Prices.--

Unique designs in new fall neckwear.

Special display now.

THE NOVEL

If possible, the novelty should be intrinsic, not simply obtruded as an attention device. In the illustrations given, this latter situation is very likely to be the case. A good example of effective and intrinsic novelty is the assertion made by the advertisements of 3-in-1 Oil: "Men shave with it." The Brownies, Gold Dust Twins, Sunny Jim, the Herpicide cards, etc., may be cited as attempts to employ the novelty device for purposes of attention.

The chief danger in using the novelty incentive is, of course, that of emphasizing the novelty rather than the product.

2. COLOR

The *use of color* for advertising purposes depends chiefly on the strong and lasting interest that all living beings have in color. The lower animals develop gorgeous plumage during the mating season, when the attention received is a chief item in the life of an individual. The savage will barter his weapons and choice possessions for bright red blankets or a chain of tinted beads. The most civilized of us loves to adorn himself with modulated hues and harmonious color schemes. Moreover, colors differ greatly in their influence. Far down in the scale of living things can be seen color preferences more or less physiological in kind. Microscopic animals are attracted by some colors, repelled by others. Bulls and frogs, with their well-known reaction to reds, illustrate the point.

The red-yellow end of the spectrum, generally

speaking, is warm and active. It is stimulating, exciting, sometimes irritating. The green-blue end, on the other hand, is cold and passive. Its action is in general depressing, quieting. To "have the blues" is a popular expression suggest-

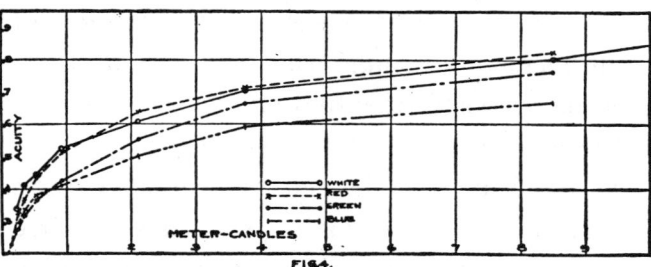

CURVES SHOWING VISUAL ACUITY WITH LIGHTS OF DIFFERENT COLORS. These curves are taken from an important study of "Visual Acuity with Lights of Different Colors and Intensities," by Dr. D. Edgar Rice, of the Department of Science and Technology of Pratt Institute. Dr. Rice remarks, "As to the effect of different colors upon acuity . . . it is quite clear that whatever differences exist are in favor of the colors at the red end of the spectrum. . . . The red and the white illuminations yield approximately equal acuity, while both are considerably higher than the green. The acuity with the blue illumination is the lowest."

ing this relation. This is more than a question of imagination and sentiment. It is a demonstrable physiological and psychological fact that the red end is dynamogenic in its influence, that is, that it increases and reinforces activities going on in the system, while the blue end inhibits. The accompanying diagram gives a set of curves showing the relative legibility of type under the same

PRINCIPLES OF APPEAL AND RESPONSE

intensity of illumination by different colors. Colors, then, if used discreetly or harmoniously, attract the eye, and, what is equally important, hold it. We do not tire of agreeable color combinations. We revel in them, contemplate them again and again, look for them on other occasions and point them out to our friends. But the colors must be properly employed or they may not only fail to hold the eye, but may actually repel it.

A significant fact is that of preferred colors. Elaborate statistical studies on men and women students in New York, Minnesota, and England disclose certain interesting differences in color preference. There is, of course, a considerable range of individual differences, and the results would be greatly modified by changes in the use to which the color might be put. Comparison of the different investigations is so interesting that I give here a summary, prepared by one of my students, of the principal results of several of them.

1. Grant Allen studied the color preferences shown by savages, securing the assistance of missionaries in various lands. He gives the following order as the result of these inquiries:

INTEREST INCENTIVES

1. Red
2. Yellow
3. Orange
4. Blue
5. Green

2. Baldwin studied the color preferences shown by a young baby, on the basis of the color reached for when variously colored papers were placed before it. He gives the following order of preferences:

1. Red
2. Blue
3. White
4. Green
5. Brown

3. Winch investigated color preferences of 2,000 school children in London, with the following order resulting, for both boys and girls:

1. Blue
2. Red
3. Yellow, falling lower with increased age and intelligence
4. Green, rising higher with increased age and intelligence

PRINCIPLES OF APPEAL AND RESPONSE

    5. White
    6. Black

4. Gordon, with only a few subjects, studied the influence of background, securing the following orders:

On Black	*On White*
1. Red	1. Blue
2. Yellow	2. Red
3. Green	3. Green
4. Blue	4. Yellow

5. Studies of students in Vassar College yield the following order of preference:

    1. Blue
    2. Red
    3. Green
    4. Yellow and Orange

6. Wissler, from his study of Columbia men and women students, deduces the following table. His results show that yellow was preferred more by the younger students than by the older. With age, he concludes, the preferred color passes on down toward the violet end of the spectrum. Combining this result with those shown in his table, we might conclude that, in so far as

INTEREST INCENTIVES

the data are reliable, the younger the person the nearer the red end of the spectrum would be his or her favorite color, and also that children and women would prefer reds, while men and older women would show greater fondness for blues.

TABLE VI
(*Wissler's Table*)

Color	Percentage of Men Who Like It	Percentage of Men Who Dislike It	Percentage of Women Who Like It	Percentage of Women Who Dislike It
Red......	22	7	42	8
Orange....	5	25	8	31
Yellow....	2	32	5	8
Green.....	7	15	9	21
Blue......	42	12	9	23
Violet.....	19	8	19	9
White.....	3	1	8	0

Taking these studies as a group, the following points are to be noted. The reds and blues stand high for educated people, the orange and yellow standing low. For children and savages just the reverse is the case. Yellow falls in the development of the race and also in the development of the individual. No very striking sex differences for order are shown, but the figures show considerable differences for amount. It is a further general principle that the most saturated colors are preferred.

Besides the strong attention value of colors, there are certain other advantages in its use which might as well be briefly enumerated while we are on the topic.

1. The use of color enables the adequate representation of the texture, quality, fabric, grain, pattern and hue of the article with less strain on the imagination.

2. It conveys a precise idea—yellow as a word may mean anything between red and blue, innumerable shades and tints of orange, yellow and yellowish green.

3. It enables the recognition of packages and articles much better than does a simple name or trade mark. The National Biscuit Company packages are good illustrations of this fact.

The value of color is illustrated by comparative tests carried on by mail-order houses in Chicago. These tests show that a cut in color often sells as high as 15 times as much as does a plain black and white cut of the same article. These houses are using more and more color in their catalogues in spite of the extra cost.

Another important fact about color which also greatly enhances its attention value is that a sign or color scheme which is really flat may be made to look solid, to have depth, to be extended in three dimensions instead of two, by the proper use of color.

Color and third dimension.—The third dimension can be suggested without the aid of perspective drawing, by simple color quality differences, in two ways.

1. By appropriate selection of brightness values. Brightness is easily taken to mean nearness, while relative dullness suggests distance. When, in the laboratory, the illumination of objects is increased or diminished, observers frequently suppose the object to be approaching or receding, although it has remained stationary throughout.

2. But the most important, practical and striking result is that secured by a proper selection of differences in hues. The red, warm end of the spectrum seems closer to us than the blue end when both really are located at the same distance. In fact, the spectral series shows an increasing suggestion of distance as we go from red and orange through yellow and green to blue and violet.

The ether waves causing the different colors are refracted by the eye in different degrees. Red

PRINCIPLES OF APPEAL AND RESPONSE

is bent least of all, yellow a little more, green still more, and blue most of all. This is the reason that a prism can break up a beam of white light into the colors of the rainbow. The waves producing the different hues emerge from the prism at different angles, so that the separate colors can be thrown upon a screen or upon the retina in the form known as the spectrum.

The following figure represents this fact:

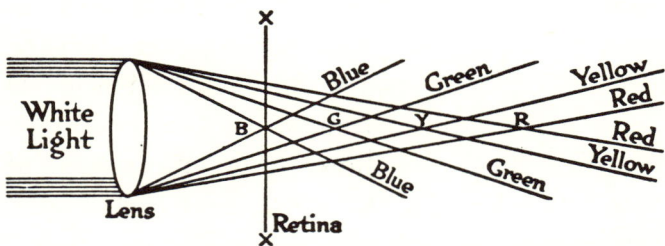

CHROMATIC ABERRATION IN THE HUMAN EYE. By way of explaining why blue and green objects seem farther away than do red and yellow objects. This principle can be used to advantage in constructing electric signs. Because of their apparent nearness the red and yellow lights stand out more prominently than the green and blue lights. (See text for explanation.)

Suppose, now, that the lens in the eye is adjusted so that the blue rays come to a focus on the retina at B and, therefore, give a clear image of the object from which they come. The red rays do not focus until R, which is some distance behind the retina. In order to get a clear picture of the red object, the lens must bulge out, becoming more convex, hence bending each ray of light correspondingly more so that the red rays focus sooner than before, until, in fact, they meet at X on the retina.

But we also bulge out this lens in order to get a clear image of a near object when we have been looking at a more distant one. In this way bulging the lens comes to mean for us a near object. And when we bulge the lens for a clear image of the red rays we naturally infer their source to be nearer. And, since we flatten the lens both for a clear picture of a distant object and for a sharp image from the blue rays, we suppose the blue object to be far away; we confuse blueness with distance.

We shall later see the appropriateness of blue for mural decorations when the suggestion of distance is desirable. The value of this principle is demonstrated in many electric light signs on our streets, though the principle is often disregarded with the result that what should seem near seems distant and vice versa. We shall take up the topic of color more fully when we consider the factors which make for sustained attention, and shall there discuss the effectiveness of different color combinations. It is sufficient here to indicate the high initial attention value of color.

PRINCIPLES OF APPEAL AND RESPONSE

3. CUTS AND ILLUSTRATIONS

Closely related to the interest in colors is that in pictures. Pictures were the first means of written communication. The letters of our alphabet can be traced far back to their early pictorial sources. The pictorial impulse is a universal one and no art has been further developed than that of pictorial representation. The reasons for this strong interest are many. Chief among them is

ILLUSTRATION AS AN ATTENTION AND INTEREST DEVICE

the fact that pictures so often afford pleasing color combinations. Again, two of the things that provoke strongest interest are personality and action. Next to a human being nothing is fuller of personality than a picture—the personality of the artist, of the subject represented, associations called up in the mind of the observer. Besides, the painter takes care to choose for his subject a

THE USE OF ILLUSTRATION

theme that has an intrinsic interest. Experiments show this pictorial interest to be stronger with women and children than men. As the race has progressed, its means of communication have developed in abstract directions, quite beyond the pictorial stage. Men who have been most active in this process seem to have lost somewhat of their earlier pictorial interest.

However, experiments go to show that there are two quite distinct classes of people in this respect, an unimaginative or imageless class, who require pictures for comprehension of statements in the copy, and another class who do not. Thus in a study by the writer of a group of expert engineers with respect to the persuasiveness of different sorts of machinery advertisements, the men broke into two sharply defined groups. Members of one group seemed to think in terms of visual pictures. They did not need an illustration of the machine, for the words themselves called up vivid mental pictures of the parts and the advantages described. To these men the presence of a cut was not necessary—they wanted all the text they could get and placed copy advertisements higher than advertisements with illustrations. But for the men in the other group the words called up no mental pictures. They seemed to think in terms of sounds and movements and had to have a complete cut of the machine before them before they could perfectly comprehend its advantages. For such men advertisements with clear cuts were more persuasive than those with

INTEREST INCENTIVES

only reading matter. See Chapter I for Table of these results.

A study by Strong of thirty women in my own laboratory showed the same two groups. This was a study of the persuasiveness of ten advertisements for a given brand of soap. In the following table the two groups are designated as Group A and Group B. The figures with the (+) or (—) indicate whether and how much these advertisements were placed above (+) or below (—) the average by the members of the two groups. The pictures represented various combinations of cuts and reading matter, and it will be seen that one group (B) consistently places cuts higher than the average, and text lower, while the other group (A) just reverses this relation, placing text higher.

TABLE VII

Groups	Character and Content of the Appeals.									
	1 All cut	2 All text	3 ½ cut	4 ¾ text	5 ½ cut	6 ½ text	7 ¾ cut	8 ¾ text	9 ¾ cut	10 All text
A	−4.2	+2.6	−0.2	+0.2	+0.7	+0.4	+1.3	−1.0	−1.0	+1.0
B	+3.1	−2.9	+0.1	−0.2	−0.3	+1.0	−1.1	+0.9	+0.5	−0.3

Averages
Group A places text advertisements high...... +1.3
Group A places cut advertisements low........ −1.0
Group B places cut advertisements high....... +1.0
Group B places text advertisements low....... −0.8

PRINCIPLES OF APPEAL AND RESPONSE

The inference is, then, that the ideal appeal should contain, other things being equal, both cut and reading matter. By this arrangement both the visual and auditory-motor types of imagination will be provided for.

Since illustrations are to be used, the question arises: What sort of a picture will be most effective? A strictly relevant cut, portraying the article itself and designed not merely to attract but to inform as well—such a cut, in fact, as the following? Or should the cut be simply a means of

A STRICTLY RELEVANT ILLUSTRATION

catching the eye—a cut more or less unrelated to the article advertised—a pretty face, a funny scene, etc., such an irrelevant cut for example as the following?

An Irrelevant Illustration

Remotely Relevant Illustration

PRINCIPLES OF APPEAL AND RESPONSE

And, since reading matter is also to be used, should it be a straightforward declaration of selling points—relevant copy?

IRRELEVANT ILLUSTRATION

Or can it be irrelevant, merely amusing, striking, or calculated to connect some special feeling with the article?

An interesting study of this question is re-

INTEREST INCENTIVES

ported by Gale. These four kinds of material were exposed for brief intervals on five different occasions and record was made of the number of times each item was observed. The results are shown by a set of curves, which show the effect of repetition on relevant and irrelevant words and cuts so far as attention value is concerned.

The chief results may be summed up as follows:

> I. With respect to attention value, the items stand in the following order:
> 1. Relevant words
> 2. Relevant and irrelevant cuts
> 3. Irrelevant words
>
> II. On five repetitions of the same appeals:
> 1. Relevant words increase in value
> 2. All cuts decrease in value
> 3. Irrelevant words do not change
>
> III. Women are more attracted by cuts and by irrelevancy than are men.

This pioneer study by Gale is a most suggestive piece of work, and its results should be checked and verified or tested by other investigations of the same kind. Such studies are now in progress in several laboratories.

PRINCIPLES OF APPEAL AND RESPONSE

4. SUGGESTED ACTIVITY

The fourth interest incentive grows out of the preceding one quite directly. It is what we may call *interest in suggested action*. Nothing is more interesting than a person, an animal, even a machine, in action. Much of the strength of window demonstrations, street vending, etc., depends on this fact. The *New York Herald* has no better advertisement than the sight of its presses, from the windows on Broadway. A barber stropping his razor, a gang of men unloading a piano, a mason using his trowel, a lather slapping in the nails, anywhere, even in politics and in the White House, the man in action attracts interest. This is not the same factor that we discerned under the head of movement. This is shown by the fact that pictures and representations of action have the same attractiveness as does the action itself. Pictures of people doing things possess an interest far greater than any representation of inert objects or the most vivid word pictures. Note the effectiveness of suggested activity as shown in the quarter-page Graphite advertisement in Chapter V.

A very curious and important fact in this connection is that to suggest action pictorially, the

INTEREST INCENTIVES

moving object must always be caught at a resting point, otherwise it suggests not action but arrest. The mistake is repeatedly made of supposing that to suggest motion, let us say of a horse trotting, the animal should be represented in the middle of its step. Nothing is further from the truth. To suggest action effectively the foot should be caught at one of two resting points, either at the initial point, before beginning the movement, or at the final point, midway between extension and return. To show it in the middle of its course suggests only pose, and stilted pose at that. Consequently walking is best represented not by a man with one foot in the air, but by one with both feet on the ground, one just having completed its swing, the other just about to begin. A man striking a blow with his fist should be represented either with an arm drawn back ready to strike or with an arm extended, the blow having been already launched, but never with it in a halfway position. Newspaper photographers are the most grievous blunderers in this respect by failing to press the button at the psychological moment. The accompanying illustrations clearly represent the truth of this principle. Compare the inertness, stiffness and lack of attractiveness in Group I with the animation and interest of Group II.

PRINCIPLES OF APPEAL AND RESPONSE

It was thought that the introduction of moving pictures and kinematograph photography would be of great service to the painter and sculptor in

The Auto may be powerless on some of our icy country roads, but the horse with

ROWE WELDED TOOL STEEL CENTER **CALKS**

goes along SURELY and SAFELY, and CAN PULL A HEAVY LOAD EASILY.

The smile of confidence on man and horse tells the story plainly—the horse has

ROWE WELDED TOOL STEEL CENTER **CALKS**

on his shoes and an otherwise nervous animal has become surefooted.

The World moves and the old-fashioned methods of horseshoe sharpening must give way to the detachable Calks

ROWE WELDED TOOL STEEL CENTER **CALKS**

Say the word and I will get a set ready

The look of satisfaction on horse and rider shows that the Captain is having an easier time of it than the men afoot; but he would not have

ARE THEY MOVING? HOW DID YOU GUESS IT?

VIOLATING THE LAW OF THE RESTING POINT. Suggestion of Pose rather than of Activity.

catching their living subjects in the process of quick action, preserving this attitude for reproduction with brush and chisel. But it was found that the expectation was all a false hope. No attitude represented action so vigorously as the

INTEREST INCENTIVES

resting points with which we were already familiar. The reason for this rather surprising circumstance is probably to be found, in part, in

THESE MOVE! DO THEY NOT?

ILLUSTRATING THE LAW OF THE RESTING POINT. Strong Suggestion of Activity.

the fact that the eye cannot perceive while it is itself in motion. Look into a mirror at your own eye, meanwhile moving the eye about. You will find yourself unable to observe the movements of your own eye. For in the moment in which the movement is taking place, the external stimulus does not have time to set up any definite images on the constantly shifting retina. So it comes that, just because we do not see the intermediate positions except when the limb is deliberately held there fixed, we do not associate them with the movement, but always the two extremes that we do see.

Observe the mental picture called up in your mind's eye when you read the words "a panther leaping." You will see the meaning is visualized either by the picture of a panther preparing to spring, or by that of a panther just alighted—probably never by the picture of a panther in the progress of the leap. Or if this should happen, you will find that the panther is at that resting point immediately between springing and landing—the point between ascent and descent, when the animal hangs poised for a moment. So a successful picture of a man leaping a fence must catch him at one of the three resting points, the moment of springing, the moment of alighting, or the moment of suspension at the height of the leap when he seems poised just above the fence.

How, then, can we represent action when there is no resting point to be caught? There are per-

INTEREST INCENTIVES

haps two chief types of cases in which this might be desirable: the case of a swiftly moving vehicle, and that of vibrating pieces of machinery. Here we clearly have a different proposition. We are dealing with inanimate objects, with mechanically produced and uniform motion. The law of association which we invoked to explain *the principle of the resting point* must also come to our assistance here. All we can do is to portray the retinal picture which the eye gets when looking at such a moving object—blurred spokes in the wheels, streaming ribbons and banners, blurred visions of oscillating levers, or what not. The law is always to put there just what the eye could really see and no more. Too much interpretation and assistance on the part of the artist defeats its own purpose.

5. THE COMIC

The use of *the comic element* as an attention incentive in business is, to say the least, precarious, and will be successful only in the most skillful hands. We may discuss this factor under three headings:

A. It must be pointed out first that the comic, while it attracts and sustains attention, draws this attention quite unto itself. The comic pictures occupying the Boston Rubber Company's advertisements attract only incidental attention to the commodity announced, and the reader remembers the picture but not the brand of goods. Repeated laboratory tests have shown this to be true.

B. As will be developed later, a statement of *selling points* is perhaps the very best direction which an appeal can take. Selling points are serious propositions, and so is the effective distribution of goods. But the introduction of levity, which usually tends toward the ridiculous in advertising copy, seems like an attempt to slur over and evade a discussion of the pertinent points at issue and to keep attention from them in favor of irrelevant material. The weakness of irrelevant matter we have already had occasion to point out.

C. One especially important characteristic of the comic is the fact that we soon become adapted to it. Jokes and funny pictures rapidly become "chestnuts" and stale. But if the comic appeal is to be employed, it is worth while knowing that the different sorts of the comic do not grow stale with equal rapidity. Reports of a prolonged experiment on the effect of repetition on the comic and on the individual differences in reaction to comic situations have already been published by the author. The full discussion can be found in the

INTEREST INCENTIVES

Psychological Review for 1911. We may divide the comic into two main types.

The rule in football is "Hit the line hard" and 'twas ours in ordering our clothing for fall. We hit the line hard and selected the finest and largest assortment of men's styles we have ever handled. It is a line that you and every man will enjoy looking through and wearing.

From $15. durability to $35. luxury, whatever quality you select you'll get the full worth of your money

To-day our special is (describe and price).

THE OBJECTIVE COMIC. The Calamity.

1. The *objective,* in which the source of amusement is the fact that some other person is involved in a predicament, is subordinated, disap-

PRINCIPLES OF APPEAL AND RESPONSE

pointed, deceived, tricked, duped or bantered, either by a third person or by natural forces,

"There ain't no such animal."
"In circus announcements we expect the unexpected—but the store that exaggerates in its advertisements is simply signalling to the sheriff."—Hubbell.

Our advertisements are so short, we're freed from the temptation of exaggeration.

Here's a suit at $15. and an overcoat at $18. where every cent of the cost has been expended to give the customers utmost values, at the prices.

THE OBJECTIVE COMIC. The Naïve.

without serious consequences. Under such circumstances we tend to be amused. The calamity joke, the naïve or unconscious joke, would be examples of this group.

INTEREST INCENTIVES

The second group, the *subjective comic,* comprises those situations in which the laugh is caused by the fact that we ourselves are tricked, surprised, discomfited mildly, disappointed, in

THE SUBJECTIVE COMIC. Play on Words.

expecting one thing, one event, one use of a word, and getting instead an unexpected one. Examples would be the pun, play on words, the sharp retort, the dialect joke, wit, etc.

Now the characteristic of the *objective comic* is that it loses its flavor rather slowly—it often waxes, increasing in funniness with repetition. The *subjective comic,* on the other hand, becomes

PRINCIPLES OF APPEAL AND RESPONSE

stale with great rapidity. When a series of comic appeals, containing examples of both classes, is arranged in an order of funniness in successive

"Signs of an early spring."
Means there's got to be something doing in our fur coats.
We have a bunch of hot ones and every one of them anxious to get in touch with YOU to prove what a warm friend it can be.
Prices $-- to $--
Fur gloves $-- to $--
Fur caps $-- to $--

THE SUBJECTIVE COMIC. Play on Words.

trials a week apart, the objective jokes rise in relative value, thus constituting a *waxing* class. The subjective appeals fall in value, thus comprising a *waning* class. Jokes which contain both ele-

INTEREST INCENTIVES

ments remain on a level. The reader is referred to the original article for further details. But the importance of this waxing and waning law, in selecting comic appeals to be repeatedly seen in an advertisement, is clear from what already has been said.

6, 7, 8. FEELING TONE, INSTINCT AND HABIT

There remain yet to be considered the interest incentives, of *feeling tone, instinctive re-*

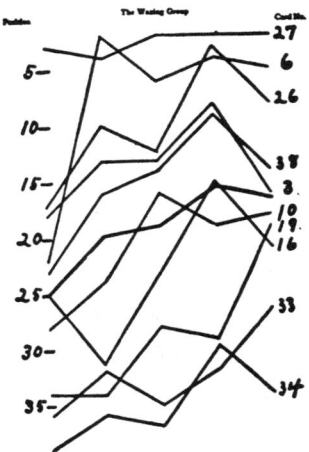

SHOWING THE INFLUENCE OF FIVE REPETITIONS ON OBJECTIVELY COMIC APPEALS. The Relative Value Increases

sponse and effective conception. While it is true that these three appeals have a strong initial at-

PRINCIPLES OF APPEAL AND RESPONSE

tention value, their greatest service lies in holding the attention already attracted by some other device, or in reinforcing the response which this appeal invited. Hence we shall treat *feeling tone*

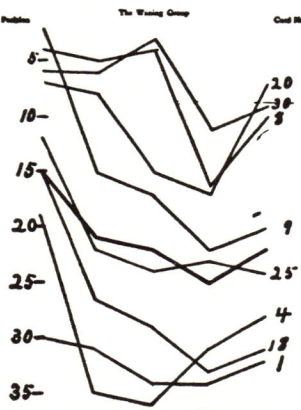

SHOWING THE INFLUENCE OF FIVE REPETITIONS ON SUBJECTIVELY COMIC APPEALS. The Relative Value Decreases

under the heading of the second task, and *instinct* and *effective conception* under the fourth task of an advertisement. But, when we come to discuss their value as "sustainers" of attention, it must be remembered that all that is said of them there applies equally well to their operation as initial appeals.

CHAPTER VII

AN EXPERIMENTAL TEST OF THE RELATIVE ATTENTION AND MEMORY VALUE OF THE MECHANICAL AND THE INTEREST DEVICES

In order to test the relative value of the *interest incentives* as compared with that of the *mechanical devices,* an interesting experiment was performed with the aid of a group of six advertising men, selected from a class which had been following a course of study based on the material presented in this book. These men were made familiar, through lectures and demonstrations, with the characteristics of the two groups of incentives. They were then given the 77 full-page advertisements found in an issue of *Everybody's Magazine,* and asked to indicate, in the case of each advertisement, the chief three incentives relied on to attract and hold attention. When less than three devices were found, the indication included only such devices as were clearly discernible. Three psychologists made similar determinations of these advertisements. The total number of votes, for the two classes of incentives, was computed for each advertisement, thus affording a fairly reliable measure of the "character" of each.

Meanwhile Dr. E. K. Strong tested the attention and memory value of each of these advertisements, as shown by the ability of 137 women to recognize them as having been previously seen in a copy of the magazine which they had had in their possession for one week, with instructions to read a certain article therein, in connection with their regular class work in college. None of these women knew that they were going to be in any way tested for their memory of the advertisements, nor, indeed, in any other way.

We have, then, the judgments of six advertising men and three psychologists on the type of incentive most prominent in each of the appeals, and these judgments are shown in the following table. We have also a measurement of the attention and memory value of each of these advertisements, as secured from the records of the 137 women readers. The following table gives these values, also. The table gives the results for the 10 best advertisements (remembered by the greatest number of readers) and for the 10 poorest (remembered by the fewest readers), exclusive of the six advertisements which appeared in preferred position (cover pages and next to reading

RELATIVE VALUE OF INTEREST DEVICES

matter). The "incentives" column gives the number of votes for each of the two types of devices.

TABLE VIII
The Ten Best Remembered

Page	Firm or Commodity Name	Number of Mechanical Incentives Reported	Number of Interest Incentives Reported	Per Cent. of 137 people who remembered
128	Ivory Soap............	6	16	8.2
6	Cosmopolitan.........	1	15	8.0
29	Barbara Worth........	1	6	8.0
117	Gillette Razor.........	8	9	7.2
37	Post Toasties.........	8	15	7.1
36	Campbell Soup........	6	17	7.1
96	Jap-a-Lac.............	5	15	6.8
66	Western Electric......	2	21	6.6
57	Baldwin Piano........	1	18	6.3
60	Mallory Hats.........	3	18	6.3
	Averages.......	4.1	15	7.2

Percentage Interest Incentives, 78.5.

The Ten Least Remembered

Page	Firm or Commodity Name	Number of Mechanical Incentives Reported	Number of Interest Incentives Reported	Per Cent. of 137 people who remembered
62	Overland Auto........	9	4	1.2
55	Genasco..............	3	13	0.9
64	Wilcox Trucks........	6	12	0.9
63	Overland Auto........	9	4	0.7
96	Dahlstrom............	2	1	0.6
48	Underfeed............	3	1	0.2
53	J. M. Asbestos........	9	9	0.2
30	Lord and Thomas.....	4	3	0.2
44	Keystone Watch......	3	5	0.0
52	Congoleum...........	5	5	0.0
	Averages.......	5.3	5.7	0.5

Percentage Interest Incentives, 51.8.

PRINCIPLES OF APPEAL AND RESPONSE

Two things are clearly indicated by the table. In the first place, those appeals which were remembered by few of the readers are the ones which utilize few definite incentives of any kind. They are the ones on which fewest votes were cast for any incentives whatsoever—they were doubtless constructed by "inspiration," without any conscious or formulated plan in mind, and they well-nigh defy analysis, either by the advertising men or by the psychologists. This is in itself a lesson worth learning.

But the second point is the one in which we are most interested in this connection. In the case of the advertisements best remembered, 78.5 per cent. of the votes were for interest incentives. These advertisements, relying for the most part on the interest devices (picture, novelty, color, feeling tone, the comic, suggested activity, instinctive reaction, and habit), are remembered by 7.2 per cent. of the 137 people, that is to say, they were remembered over 14 times as often as were those relying on mechanical devices.

In the case of these latter advertisements, the average amount of mechanical incentive (5.3) is even a little more than in the case of those of the first group. The only considerable change is in the degree to which interest incentives are relied

RELATIVE VALUE OF INTEREST DEVICES

on. Here we find only 51.8 per cent. of the votes given to interest incentives, as contrasted with the 78.5 per cent. in the case of the better group. And, indeed, even this fairly high per cent. is almost entirely due to two of the appeals.

Taking the appeals one by one, in the case of the 10 best remembered ones, without exception, the interest incentives predominate. In the case of the 10 least remembered, in 7 cases out of the 10 the mechanical incentives either equal or exceed the interest incentives, leaving only 3 in which the reverse is the case.

The superiority of the interest incentives, for purposes of attention and memory, for which we have contended throughout this discussion, is most thoroughly confirmed by the results of this experiment, as well as by the returns from advertisements actually run.

CHAPTER VIII

THE SECOND TASK: HOLDING THE ATTENTION

Let us assume, now, that, through the application of some principle in the foregoing chapters, an appeal has been formed so as to attract initial attention. The final effectiveness of the appeal will depend on whether or not this attention can be *held* long enough for the suggestion or the argument to take its place in consciousness along with other appeals and to modify the later responses of the reader. This is the point at which the persuasiveness of the appeal first begins to make itself felt. Persuasion is simply the act of *holding the favorable attention* long enough for the stimulus to enter into effective combination with other processes in consciousness. Such combination leads to the response. What the response is will be determined partly by the needs, resources and general purposes of the reader. But it depends also largely upon the character of the appeal, for this appeal may be potent enough

HOLDING THE ATTENTION

to create his needs, suggest resources, and modify his general purposes.

We have already seen that *attention always fluctuates* or comes in pulses. The appeal then cannot operate by simply prolonging the first moment of attention. It must be so constructed that after this first moment the eye does not move to another thing, but fixates again and again the original object, that is to say, the reader must be able to see some new phase or aspect in the original appeal. Figure 1 (page 134) is able to hold attention, but it does so by appearing to change its character. Now it is seen as a stairway leading upward, now it is a stairway upside down, now a set of steps seen from below, now from above, etc. As fast as attention to one aspect wanes another aspect suggests itself. The same is true of figures 2 and 3. Watch a passenger reading the Subway advertisements. You will see at once that he hurries by some cards and lingers over others. Or compare your own interest in the following advertisements. The first is too simple, the second is too complex and choppy, while the third is in some way so constructed that you look at it again and again; it holds your attention. What then are the requisites for sustained attention?

PRINCIPLES OF APPEAL AND RESPONSE

Here again we may point out two groups of factors, a group of mechanical devices and a group of interest devices.

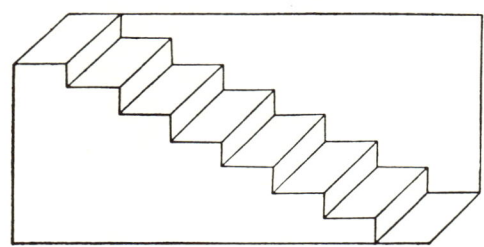

FIGURE 1

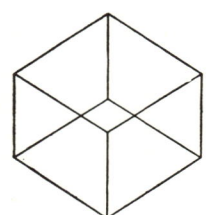

FIGURE 2

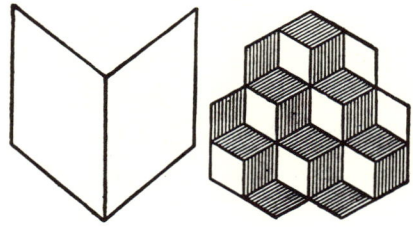

FIGURE 3

FIGURES APPEARING TO CHANGE CHARACTER

HOLDING THE ATTENTION

I. MECHANICAL HELPS

1. *Complexity.*—Unless the advertisement is intended to be a mere reminder, a mere suggestion

CARDS FROM NEW YORK SUBWAY

of some other appeal previously seen, a certain amount of complexity is requisite. The advertisement should contain shifting points so that,

PRINCIPLES OF APPEAL AND RESPONSE

while attention must fluctuate, it can flit from point to point, aspect to aspect, of the same space. Perhaps three elements or units, three facts, styles, etc., represent the ideal; three arguments or propositions of interest, three figures if the advertisement takes the form of picture, three styles or sizes of type, three color masses, etc.

Securing Unity through Structure

This allows one object for the focus, one for the field, and one for the margin, and, if the elements are properly unified, prevents the encroachment of parts of some foreign unit into consciousness.

2. *Unity.*—The second mechanical factor then is that of *unity*. Not only must there be complexity, but the elements should be so interrelated as to form a whole, so related that the shift from one to the other is perfectly natural. There are

various ways in which this unity can be accomplished.

(a) *Structure.*—The elements may all participate in a general design or composition, as do the figures in the Arrow Collar card. By the direction in which the faces are turned, by some common act in which all are engaged, etc., attention may be led from point to point in the total composition, and always returned, in the long run, to the salient points or center of the arrangement. Notice how all the lines and all the faces of all the figures are turned in the direction of the man with the collar in the Arrow collar card. The Sistine Madonna is the classical example of such an arrangement. Aside from these devices of composition, the *content* of the parts may all assist in the formation of a unit. Thus a question may lead naturally to an answer which follows or is to be found in another part of the composition.

(b) *The use of pointers, curves, arrows, borders and similar lines* may also be used to the same end. The *border* gives an artificial unity to the contents bounded by it. It tends to keep the eye within the given area, since the eye reflexly tends to follow lines rather than to leap across them. Just as the pasture fence keeps the cattle wandering about the enclosure instead of

PRINCIPLES OF APPEAL AND RESPONSE

breaking out of it, so the *border*, the *curve*, the *pointer*, keep the restless eye from straying to foreign quarters by turning it ever back toward the center of the composition. Moreover these borders, frames and lines of demarcation may be

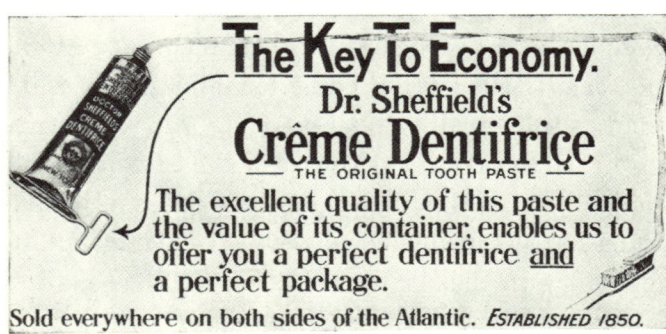

AN ATTEMPT TO SECURE UNITY BY MECHANICAL MEANS (Lines)

themselves artistically designed and so possess positive attention value which may reinforce that of the content of the space which they embrace. The simple law that the eye tends to move *along* lines instead of across them is worth bearing in mind.

II. INTEREST DEVICES

The mechanical devices for sustaining attention should not be disregarded, but their importance is insignificant as compared with what we may call the *feeling tone* of the appeal itself. By *feel-*

HOLDING THE ATTENTION

ing tone we mean the *pleasantness* or *unpleasantness* which accompanies our perception of objects. Every object in our experience has a twofold character. It is at once an object of *cognition* and an object of *feeling.*

From the point of view of cognition it is this or that object, has this or that use, is made of this or that material, and so on. From the other point of view it is not only this or that kind of object, but it also makes us feel agreeable or disagreeable, comfortable or uncomfortable in its presence. It makes us feel either desire or aversion, it either attracts or repels. Experiments show that we not only *feel* at the same time that we *perceive,* but that we also make characteristic movements toward the object.

The *feeling of pleasantness* is accompanied by *expansive, open, appropriative* bodily attitudes, and by actual movements toward the agreeable stimulus. Under these conditions stimuli effect easy entrance to the higher levels, make strong impressions and are long remembered. The *pleasant impression tends to persist* in consciousness, long after the original stimulus has been removed.

The *feeling of unpleasantness,* on the contrary, is accompanied by *retractile, conflicting or evasive* movements, the organism tends to shrink away from the stimulus rather than to move towards it. Under these conditions the resistance of the nervous pathways is increased, stimuli make relatively faint impression, and this impression tends easily to oblivisce or be forgotten. Along with the law of persistence of the pleasant goes that of *the obliviscence of the disagreeable*.[1] The importance of the feeling tone of an appeal ought, then, to be very apparent. The feeling tone of an advertisement, as of any other object, will influence not only the amount of attention it receives but its persistence in consciousness as well, and it follows that the reaction to the appeal will also involve the article in the interest of which the appeal is made.

The feeling tone of an appeal may depend on two principal factors:

I. On its form or arrangement, its character as a work of art, its general beauty. Symmetry, proportion, clearness, balance, the quality of lines, spaces, masses, colors, harmonies, atmosphere, all play their rôle here, all of those elements and laws of design which a course on the "Principles of Arrangement" would treat.

II. The feeling tone will depend not only on the

---

[1] See the article on this subject, by the writer, in the *Journal of Philosophy, Psychology and Scientific Methods*, Dec. 22, 1910.

form of the appeal but on its content as well. Words have their feeling tone just as do lines and color. Besides, certain objects, ideas, topics, people, purposes, characteristics, arguments, associations, etc., have the power to arouse strong agreeable feeling on the part of the reader while others are intrinsically repulsive.

CHAPTER IX

FEELING TONE OF FORM

These factors I shall discuss under the headings of the various elements of design—lines, form, relations, masses, colors, harmonies, etc.

LINES

Mathematically, lines are lacking in quality as they are in width, but psychologically, even the simplest line, as it appears in sketching, has both feeling tone and symbolic significance. This feeling tone of lines can be utilized to advantage in representing advertised articles by both relevant and irrelevant cuts, and should also be considered in the appropriate selection of type faces. The feeling tone of a line depends upon three chief factors: (1) its quality; (2) its direction; (3) its character, as straight or curved.

Quality.—The factors constituting the quality of a line are: (1) breadth; (2) intensity; (3) texture; (4) color. By these we mean: (1)

whether the line is wide or narrow; (2) dark or light; (3) rough or smooth; (4) its hue.

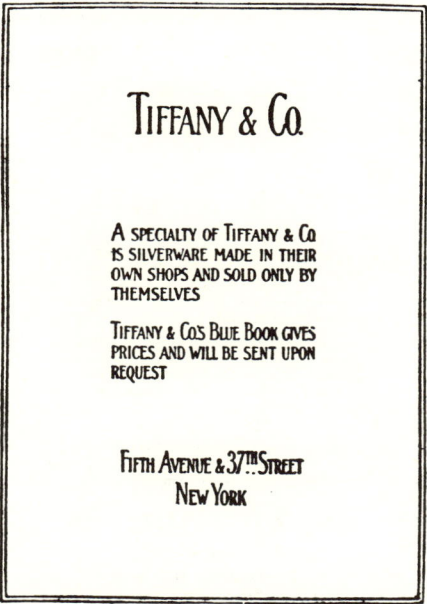

THE FINE BLACK LINE, SUGGESTING PRECISION AND HARDNESS

Speaking generally, the following principles hold:

> The fine gray line suggests delicacy of texture.
> The fine black line suggests precision and hardness.
> The broad rough line suggests homeliness and solidity.

PRINCIPLES OF APPEAL AND RESPONSE

The proper selection of lines in cuts or copy is of great utility in showing the texture of the article, or in lending atmosphere either to the cut, the object, or the appeal as a whole.

> ## Solid Silver
> for
> ## Wedding Gifts
>
> The productions in Silver now displayed in the warerooms of The Gorham Company form an interesting exposition of the highest achievements in the art of silversmithing in this period of its greatest development.
>
> The collection is not approached elsewhere in quality and variety of complete sets and individual pieces, but while it is so comprehensive it has been so carefully and conveniently arranged that your invited inspection may be made without confusion or waste of energy.
>
> Choice also may be exercised within an extensive range as to article, pattern or cost, with equal freedom from trouble or embarrassment.
>
> ## The Gorham Co.
> **Silversmiths**
> **5th Avenue & 36th Street**
> 17 and 19 Maiden Lane

THE BROAD BLACK LINE, SUGGESTING SOLIDITY AND WEIGHT

Direction.—1. Verticals.—The moderate use of vertical lines conveys a suggestion of simplicity, firmness and dignity, with a certain severe grace. Excess of verticals, however, is likely to give stiffness and rigid formality.

There are two psychological reasons for this effect of verticals:

FEELING TONE OF FORM

(a) The feeling tone of all spatial elements, as of many spatial arrangements, depends on imitative tendencies to movement or attitude which they provoke on the part of the observer. The instinctive response to a vertical line consists in straightening out the body, assuming an erect position. This is the position we assume in moments of formality, sternness, attention, dress

ILLUSTRATING APPROPRIATE USE OF HORIZONTAL LINES

parade, etc., and hence at once suggests to us the emotions accompanying these movements.

(b) Ideal literary and architectural associations of towers, monuments, columns, warriors, etc., with their erect, proud direction, have come to make the vertical symbolic of "uprightness," moral strength, and this symbolism still attaches itself to such a line, even when it is in no sense a part of the object with which the original association was made.

2. Horizontals.—The movement from side to

side is the movement which the eye can execute with the least effort. So much is this true that we overestimate the length of verticals as compared with equal horizontals, since the former require so much effort for the eye to sweep along them from end to end. Side to side movements are frequent, as in sweeping the horizon, reading, looking at an audience, etc. Their very frequency

ILLUSTRATING INAPPROPRIATE USE OF DIAGONAL LINES

is probably the chief reason for their relatively greater ease. Hence the horizontal is the line of ease, quiescence and repose, almost of languor, ''the suggestion of lying down and the consequent suggestion of quiet and relaxation being particularly strong.''

As is well known, the headpiece of the Roman cross must be actually shorter if it is to appear equal to the arm pieces. The extra effort involved in running the eye along the vertical head piece makes that line seem equal in length to the

FEELING TONE OF FORM

actually longer but more easily perceived horizontal arm.

3. Diagonals.—The diagonal line seems to the observer to be full of action and movement. The psychological reasons for its possession of this character are:

(a) The fact that our bodies when engaged in tense action of effort or movement are thrown into such oblique lines in order to counterbalance load or resistance. Hence, when we see these diagonals, we associate the direction with the oblique lines which we observe when human beings are active.

(b) The diagonal sets up imitative movements on the part of the observer. We tend to throw our own body in a direction corresponding to that of the line, and these movements at once call up the feelings of strain and activity associated with them under other circumstances. The "Gladiator Combatant" in the Louvre and the diagonal of the three figures running, suggests this rush and speed of the oblique line generally. So does St. Gaudens' bas-relief on Boston Commons, and the Winged Victory fragment.

4. Curves.—Generally speaking, curves are more pleasing than straight lines, whether the curve be arc, serpentine, loop, spiral or what not. The

PRINCIPLES OF APPEAL AND RESPONSE

reason for this preference for curves is not very clear. The old theory that the most natural and agreeable eye movement was such as would be

FEELING TONE FROM DIRECTION OF LINES

made in following the preferred curves has been shown to be false. The eye, even in following curves, exerts jerky and irregular movements, which when traced or photographed do not at all make æsthetic lines. The most probable explanation is that offered by Gordon that "the curve suggests smooth and easy movement in other parts of the body. We are able to move hand, wrists, head and feet, at least in serpentine lines and to experience the greatest ease and pleasure as well as the greater economy and power of these movements. It seems fair to assume that the memory of these movements, and perhaps some actual half-conscious movements like them, may be the basis of our æsthetic appreciation of the serpentine line.''

At any rate, curves, whether they occur in copy, cut or decorative design, avoid the hardness and stiffness likely to be produced by straight lines, giving an atmosphere of grace, pliability, richness and voluptuousness.

CLOSED FORMS

Geometrical forms, as well as lines, have their own individual feeling tone due (1) to the character of their boundary lines and (2) to the character of the enclosed space. The chief source of these qualities seems again to be imitative movements or memories on our own part.

1. *The triangle* with its diagonal lines and sharp corners is lively, incisive and delicately balanced. Especially if it be not resting on its base, it is strongly suggestive of spirit, life and con-

stant motion. The stars themselves are not really five-pointed, but nothing represents their twinkling better than a combination of triangles. Triangles would form an appropriate border for advertisements of sparkling water, wine, lively music, light, etc. An isosceles triangle resting on its base is a perfect example of balance that is not dead but quite alive and active.

2. *The square,* composed as it is of vertical and horizontal lines, unites at once the stiffness and firmness of the former with the ease and repose of the latter, hence suggests solidity and strength, sturdiness. This is true so long as the square remains on one of its sides. The moment it stands on one corner it resolves itself into triangles and conveys the corresponding impression of delicate balance and liveliness.

3. *The Oblong.*—These forms vary so much in proportion and magnitude that it is difficult to assign them as a class any common emotional quality. But one interesting and important feature about them is the fact of rather decided preference for certain proportions. Nearly a hundred years ago Zeising argued for the "golden section" as the most beautiful of all proportions. By the "golden section" is meant a division of a whole into two parts, in such a relation that the

FEELING TONE OF FORM

size of the whole is to the size of the larger part as that part is to the smaller ($a + b : a :: a : b$), or, roughly, a ratio between the two parts of 3:5. The law was supposed to hold for the division of lines and rectangles, dimensions of rectangles, ellipses, and other geometrical forms, as well as for concrete objects of art and industry, rooms, blocks, playing cards, windows, doors, fountains, books, writing paper, etc.

In order to be most pleasing, the dimensions of these objects must conform to the 3:5 ratio. There has since been considerable experimental evidence for this preference, and the measurement of many forms which are pleasing will be found to conform to it. Advertisements should utilize all possible chances of pleasing the eye. The division of the advertisement into cut and copy, the size of the card or space, the shape of trade marks, etc., could all utilize the principle, and doubtless with good effect. But it should be remarked here that the apparent proportion of a closed space form is often modified by the influence of adjacent elements and figures and the rôle which the form plays in the design as a whole. So much for the lines and forms. Let us now turn to the matter of relations, or to what are called the principles of design.

PRINCIPLES OF APPEAL AND RESPONSE

PRINCIPLES OF DESIGN

The general laws of arrangement will be found fully analyzed in text books on design and decoration, and somewhat more briefly in the text books on æsthetics, but it seems worth while to sum up a few of these principles in the present connection. So far as we shall do this, the matter will fall under the three heads of rhythm, balance and stability.

1. *Rhythm* is an important element in agreeable decoration, such as borders, etc. The basis of rhythm lies in the motor response, of an imitative kind, which the observer makes. The body is a rhythmical machine, and repetitions that fall in with organic rhythm easily fall into rhythmical groupings in perception.

Rhythm consists of some kind of repetition, but this repetition need not be literal nor complete. The essential thing about rhythm in spatial design is that the *direction of the movement* be (1) definite and (2) clearly indicated.

does not produce a rhythmical effect, but—

FEELING TONE OF FORM

B

does, since it reads clearly from left to right. The single element gives direction, and the design as a whole is but a repetition of this motive. In A the movement may be either left-right or right-left, hence A cannot be called a rhythmical design. But there may be subdivision of the element, so that some larger section of the design serves as the motive.

Thus in

C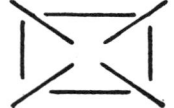

there is repetition more or less complete, but only the group of four elements suggests direction, hence the group would be the element of rhythm. This is also true in the case of D.

D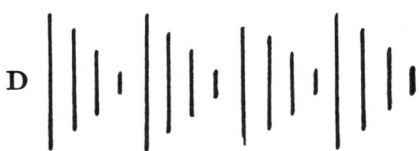

2. *Balance in Design.*—Just as balance is necessary in color arrangement, so it is an essential

factor in spatial arrangement. The human body is bilaterally symmetrical, and designs which set up bi-symmetrical movements of examination, response or imitation fit in most agreeably with the organic habit and structure. The most perfect balance would be what we call bilateral symmetry. In such compositions each half is a perfect copy of the other except for direction. Only in very formal compositions can this condition be conformed to. In actual representative painting, in type arrangement and illustrations by cuts, some deviation is of course required.

So for practical purposes we usually have to resort to what Puffer calls "substitutional symmetry." According to the principles of "substitutional symmetry" there are four items of "weight" in composition, and these four items may be made to balance each other in various combinations. The items are:

1. Mass.
2. Depth or vista.
3. Direction (of line or motion or attention).
4. Interest.

Says Gordon: "In good pictures one will probably find an equation in which two of these items are set over against the other two, unless

FEELING TONE OF FORM

BALANCE OF MASS AGAINST VISTA (Distance)

it happens that one item is extraordinarily stronger, and in this case it will be balanced by the other three. In a portrait, for instance, if the mass of the person's form is on one side of the

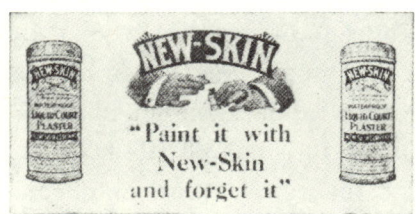

MECHANICAL BALANCE OF MASS AGAINST MASS

canvas, together with some interesting object, like a flower or an animal, one would expect to find on the opposite side some vista of depth or direction of attention by means of line or motion."

PRINCIPLES OF APPEAL AND RESPONSE

In this substitutional symmetry a small, interesting object is found to balance a larger but less interesting one.

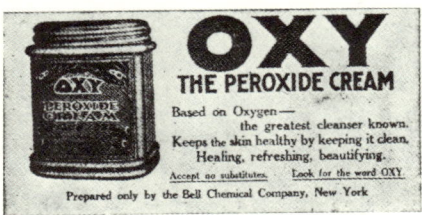

DISREGARDS THE LAW OF BALANCE

3. *Stability.*—Here we may again quote Gordon: "Another phase of the problem of balance is the distribution of masses and space between the upper and lower parts of a composition. An arrangement may be symmetrical on its right and left halves, but wholly unsymmetrical as between upper and lower halves. In general, to prevent top-heaviness and give, as it were, enough ballast to a composition, there should be more below the center than above it. Pierce's experiments show that the principle of stability is even of more moment than that of left and right balance. An inverted pyramid would be an unpleasant and precarious-looking structure. The visible sign of a sure equilibrium is breadth of base, and most massive things are built to slope by more or less obvious degrees toward their tops.

FEELING TONE OF FORM

It is not true, though, that all beautiful and well-poised forms are larger at the bottom; very good effects are sometimes secured by putting the mass of the thing represented near the upper limit of the picture. A mass of graceful flowers may fill the upper part with only their slender stocks below; a drift of clouds or a flock of birds may be shown high up in the picture, with only a few landscape lines below, the nearest approach to empty space. Why do not such pictures look as top-heavy and unstable as the inverted pyramid?

"The reason is that they represent things that are not dead, inanimate weights, but are delicate and light. Placing the flowers or clouds or birds above the center of the picture, with the empty space below, is just what suits their character, and brings out their lightness and buoyancy. These two facts, then, are part of the same truth; to gain stability, large masses must be below the center, and this is appropriate when the masses are supposed to be heavy; to gain freedom and buoyancy, masses may lie above the center, and this is appropriate when the masses represent something light."

CHAPTER X

FEELING TONE OF CONTENT

Under this heading come the topics: color quality, color harmony and balance, relations of feeling tone to imagination, imagery types, feeling tone of words, pictures and associations, and the curious facts of synæsthesia. These topics we now take up in order.

CHARACTER OF COLORS

To sensitive observers the simple colors, taken separately, possess different emotional tones. This tone depends partly on the physiological factors already discussed, and partly on associations which may have been originally of a more or less arbitrary kind. On this point I can do no better than quote from Gordon's "Æsthetics" (p. 146).

1. *Red.*—"Red has been compared to the blare of a trumpet, loud and ringing; it is also known as one of the 'warm' colors. Some clue to the emotional effect of a color is gained by a glance

FEELING TONE OF CONTENT

at the associations and the symbolism which have grown up around it. Red, the color of the blood, is the symbol of passion and death. Among the Chinese it is said to denote virtue and truth. With the ancient Romans the red flag was the battle signal. In the middle ages of Europe the candidate for knighthood was invested with the red garment in token of his readiness to shed his blood. In the Christian era Christ and the Virgin are very generally represented as wearing a red tunic under a blue mantle. The symbolic use of red in modern art is illustrated in Rossetti; in 'Dante's Dream' the angel of love is all in scarlet and scarlet poppies strew the floor, and in 'Beata Beatrix' there is the scarlet dove. A distinction was made, in religious art, between different qualities of the same color; for example, a clear red denoted a pure feeling, but a muddy red was the hue of sin. In Abbey's 'Holy Grail' paintings the robe of Gallahad is a clear red.''

2. *Yellow.*—''The yellow of the spectrum is the brightest of all the spectral hues. It is joyous and uplifting; in the orient a sacred color, a symbol of faith and of the sun. The Christian church, however, made yellow the color of dishonor, and in popular symbolism it stands for jealousy and decay. Pale yellow and gold are among the most

adaptable colors in the sense of making pleasant combinations with almost any other color. Both red and yellow are usually spoken of as strong or exciting colors, though the type of excitement is not the same in both. Red is said to suggest a hurried, onward, dashing, but orderly movement, accompanied by sound; yellow a lighter, airy, whirling movement."

3. *Green.*—"Green belongs to the cool end of the spectrum, and is less exciting than the reds and yellows. Grant Allen points out that green is, among primitive peoples, relatively unprized. He says the men in civilized communities, i.e., in cities, have missed the green of the fields and woods, and hence have come to the appreciation of it. In Christian symbolism it stands for hope and inspiration. We connect it also with springtime and growing things."

4. *Blue.*—"Blue is generally felt to be cool and calm and to be suggestive of stillness and depth. Ruskin writes as follows: 'Wherever Turner gives blue, there he gives atmosphere; it is air, not object. Blue he gives to his sea, so does nature; blue he gives, sapphire deep, to his eternal distance, so does nature; blue he gives to the mighty shadows and hollows of his hills—but blue he gives not where detailed and illumined surfaces

are visible.' Lafcadio Hearn writes similarly and says that blue appeals to one's ideas of 'altitude, of vastness and of profundity,' and that it is the 'tint of distance and vagueness.' And again, 'Vivid blue, unlike other bright colors, is never associated in our experience of nature with large opaque solidity.'

"Blue tones, thus, since they are enveloping, atmospheric and spacious, should be proper for the decoration of backgrounds, of walls and of ceilings. The beautiful fitness of Puvis de Chavannes' mural paintings is due in part to their soft prevailing blues. Blue in Christian art and in popular symbolism is the color for constancy."

5. *White, Gray and Black.*—"White stimulates a joyful but serene mood. It is the symbolic color of joy and purity. Gray is of all colors the most sober, quiet and subtle. A laboratory subject, whose task was to look at a large sheet of gray paper and to record her impression of the color experience, wrote as follows: 'Visually a pure gray, it gives the impression of softness and depth. I seem to hear its very quietness. Its gentleness of gradation and of shading suggests grace, delicacy, and expertness. The whole experience is one of neatness, delicacy, and refine-

PRINCIPLES OF APPEAL AND RESPONSE

ment, which ideas produce a bodily feeling of reverence or of deference.'"

Poetically we find gray referred to as a "chastened tinge" or as ashen or sober.

Black by itself is melancholy and depressing, it is the symbol, among western peoples, of grief and death. It stands also for quiet. In combination with other colors, particularly when it is limited in extent, black makes the impression of great concentration and strength. No other color has more "character" than black.

COLOR COMBINATIONS

Without going into the technical aspect of color mixture or of decorative design we may give several leading principles of agreeable color combinations:

1. Cool colors harmonize well with their own tints, but tints of warm colors usually harmonize best with other colors, or with their own shades.

2. Complementary colors combine agreeably, but combinations of colors not quite complementary (leaning toward the warm end) are usually preferred.

3. Oranges and yellows and golds have the most acceptable harmonizing qualities, and they com·

bine well both with their own shades and with other colors. Even discordant colors can often be reconciled by joining their edges with a band of gold.

4. For the most part, colors combine pleasantly with the white-gray-black series. But it seems that the better a color harmonizes with other colors, the less pleasing is it in combination with gray.

5. The most agreeable combinations, according to Kirschmann, are those which exhibit three kinds of contrast effect, namely: Contrast of hue, of brightness and saturation.

6. For brilliant and vivacious effects the contrasted color scheme is the best suited. "This would show, perhaps, two key colors, whose tints and shades would weave together, or, according to some, a concentrated scheme must represent the three colors red, blue and yellow" (Gordon, p. 151).

7. For a more uniform and subdued effect the gradual transition of the dominant method is better suited. Here "there should be one prevailing hué, and variations should be introduced by changes in the saturation and brightness and by limited changes in hue. There might be touches of contrasted colors, but not enough to interfere

PRINCIPLES OF APPEAL AND RESPONSE

with the impression of a single governing hue" (Gordon, p. 151).

COLOR BALANCE

1. *Quantity* (From Gordon, p. 153).—"When two masses of color are alike in every way, hue, brightness, saturation, size, shape—occupying symmetrical positions on either side of a picture or design—they are said to balance. In this figurative conception of balance the center of the picture is regarded as a fulcrum and the horizontal distances out from the center are the two arms of the lever. We know that in maintaining a literal physical balance, if we shorten the arm of a lever on one side we must increase the weight on that side, but that if we lengthen the arm we must diminish the weight. The same thing is true of the apparent balance between color masses. A small color mass far out from the center balances a large mass close up to the center. A more complex problem presents itself when the two opposed colors are no longer of the same quality; when, for instance, blue must be balanced with orange, or yellow with green. Experiments show that (on a dark background) a small mass of bright color seems to balance a large mass of dull color. If, then, we had a bright and a dark

mass of equal size the bright mass should be put on the shorter lever arm, that is, nearer the center of the picture, since its extra weight must be offset by short leverage. . . . On a light background the more a color approaches black the greater its weight or value.''

2. *Quality.*—Besides this quantitative balance, there is a balance of quality depending on the phenomenon of contrast. According to Ross (''A Theory of Pure Design''), ''Tones, simply as tones, disregarding the positions, measures, and shapes which may be given to them, balance, when the contrasts which they make with the ground tone upon which they are placed are equal.''

Says Gordon: ''When a composition contains three or more hues, then a balance becomes possible. In a design of white, gray, and black the brightnesses balance when the gray is as much darker than the white as the black is darker than the gray. The hues of yellow, greenish yellow and orange yellow would balance if the greenish and the orange yellows were removed by equal degrees from pure yellow. It is also proper to speak of a balance of saturations when two tones vary by equal degrees of saturation from a ground tone.''

PRINCIPLES OF APPEAL AND RESPONSE

So much for the *feeling tone of form and arrangement*. It is impossible in the time at our disposal to illustrate each of these facts in the concrete field of advertising. The composer or designer must himself make the applications. But the propriety or impropriety of a given form ought to be fairly obvious if the foregoing principles are borne in mind. Thus the writer recalls an advertisement for beds and mattresses in which the composer sought to convey an atmosphere of quiet and repose. But the effect was utterly destroyed by the insistent activity of a diagonal line of type and contrasting color which ran across the composition. Moreover, the colors selected for this appeal were not the quieting and soothing blues and greens, but aggressive and irritating oranges and yellows. The best way to realize fully the importance of these laws of feeling tone is to go about looking for examples of their violation.

The lines, forms, relations, colors and distribution of elements should so far as possible reflect the character of the goods or the mood desired in the reader. A patent illustration of this would be the fact that in selecting type faces, bulk, weight, mass or strength demands heavy, strong, bold faced type, while an appeal to feeling or emo-

FEELING TONE OF CONTENT

HARMONIOUS COÖRDINATION BETWEEN SUBJECT, TYPE AND TRADE-MARK

tion should be conveyed by means of artistically formed letters, shaded type, with free, flowing or graceful lines. Observe the accompanying il-

Lord & Taylor

Imported Lace Curtains

Arab   Marie Antoinette   Renaissance
Brussels   Irish Point

600 pairs at . . *$12.50* pair
Value $15.00 and $18.50

325 pairs at   *$17.50* pair
Value $21.50 and $25.50

*Point Arab and Italian Filet
Lace Curtains*
at *$35.00, 50.00, 75.00, 115.00* pair
Usual prices $50.00, $65.00, $100.00, $150.00

Embroidered Portieres
Single pairs
Formerly $40.00 to $110.00 pair
at *$20.00 to 65.00* pair

Broadway & 20th St.; 5th Ave.; 19th St.

TYPE FACES SUGGESTING REFINEMENT AND DELICACY OF TEXTURE

lustrations, which show the effectiveness of such selection.

FEELING TONE AND IMAGINATION

The feeling tone of a given composition of reading matter and cut will also depend somewhat on what is called the imagery type of the reader. We can think of objects even when they are not present to our sense organs. Thus I can call up in my mind's eye more or less vividly my boyhood home, and seem to see, though more obscurely than if I were present on the spot, the house and barn, the grape arbor, the garden, even my little bookcase in the library. I can smell the honey in the bee boxes and can hear the general hum and stir of the hives. I can do this because I can call up images of these past experiences. Or by putting together the images of wheels, sails, birds, ropes, etc., which I have actually seen in the past, I can create in my mind's eye an aeroplane of a pattern which has never yet been constructed.

Similarly, if you read the following list of words through slowly, you will find that each word calls up some *image* of the thing it represents.

FEELING TONE OF CONTENT

Violin	Earthquake
Beefsteak	Falling from a balloon
Subway	Battle
Cheese	Caruso
Surf	Elevator

You will find, further, that some of the images come quickly, others slowly; some are strong and vivid, others faint or obscure; some words will call up visual pictures, some auditory, others feelings of movement, still others tastes, smells, touches, temperatures, etc. You will likely find that in your own case the swift and vivid images will all tend to be of the same type: visual, auditory, etc., as the case may be.

But if you compare your results with those of several of your friends you will likely find striking differences. One will think of "earthquake" in terms of rumbling noises, another in terms of irregular and sudden tossings and movements of his own body, while still another will see falling buildings, smoke, and frightened people in his mind's eye. With respect to their normal and most vivid imagery, people show not universals but types. And the result of such an experiment as that above will usually reveal the imagery type of the reader, that is, it will show what kinds of

PRINCIPLES OF APPEAL AND RESPONSE

imagery he employs easily, quickly, vividly and most frequently.

Thus one observer recorded 2,500 of his own images during two years of study of the subject, and recorded the following table:

TABLE IX

Visual............57%	Organic........... 1%
Auditory..........20%	Taste............. 6%
Olfactory.......... 6%	Motor............ 3%
Tactual........... 4%	Emotional......... 1%
Temperature....... 2%	

The two types that are most pronounced are the *visual* type and the *auditory-motor* type.

Images of the so-called "lower senses," touch, taste, smell, temperature, etc., are both slow and weak as well as infrequent with most people. But in describing such things as clothing, furniture, food products, toilet articles, fabrics, soaps, perfumes, etc., the advertiser desires very much to arouse such images. If they can be aroused successfully, they not only add tremendous interest to the advertisement itself, but they may actually constitute selling points for the article described. This will be especially true of all appeals made over the *short circuit*—all appeals to the appetite, the instincts, the feelings and emotions of the prospective purchaser. And it is precisely with such articles as those mentioned above that the

FEELING TONE OF CONTENT

feeling appeal seems to be most effective—**articles** which contribute toward personal **comfort, convenience, pleasure and satisfaction, and which yet** do not involve any great expenditure. It **is well,** then, to point out the ways in which these **images** may be most effectively aroused.

1. *Words.*—It is difficult to arouse **images of** touch, taste, smell, temperature, appetite, etc., **by** means of *words*. But it can be accomplished **if** the words are chosen carefully for their **poetic** quality and applied with a certain moderate profusion and cumulative effect. The poetic qualities of words depend on two chief **factors.**

(a) Their phonic composition.—Certain combinations of oral sounds are in themselves **agreeable,** and the advertising writer should develop **a** delicate sense for the feeling tone **of sound combinations.** Compare, for instance, **the auditory** distastefulness of the words in the **first column** with the agreeableness of those in the **second.**

I	II
Tootsie Rolls	Sapolio
Lemon Squash	Ivory
Waw-waw Sauce	Electroline
Bootz Cordial	Clover Farms
Beakes Dairy	Crystal Domino
Stink	Spearmint
Foot-Eazer	Shakamaxon

PRINCIPLES OF APPEAL AND RESPONSE

This matter of phonic feeling tone can be best studied by using words in a foreign language, whose meanings are unknown. The elements of association and poetic usage are thus eliminated, and striking results are secured. Thus a French woman is reported as having said that "cellar door" is the most pleasing of English words.

(b) Besides arousing the feeling tone due to phonetic composition, words may be pleasant or unpleasant because of *associations* which cluster around them. These associations are largely due to literary usage, though this usage will usually be found to depend on simple psychological facts due to the quality, composition, origin or history of the words themselves. Thus there tends to be, on the whole, a certain set of words which, while conversationally satisfactory, are felt to be inappropriate for use in literary composition. And even in the language of writing, as distinct from language of conversation, certain words and groups of words seem to be sacred to poetry, romance and song. Compare, with this idea in mind, the two following columns of words.

I	II
Horse	Steed
Girl	Maiden

FEELING TONE OF CONTENT

Writing	Scripture
Book	Volume
Candy	Sweet-meat
Jump	Leap
Hogs	Swine
Light	Ignite

The factors involved here are too complex for brief discussion. It must suffice to point out that the image-power of words depends largely on their feeling tone. An appreciation of this feeling tone must come from literary training rather than from scientific experiment.

2. *Pictures.*—A peculiar thing about these images from the lower senses is that, although they are not easily aroused directly by words, they come rather easily and vividly when a visual image or impression is present to help them into consciousness. Consequently, the most effective way of producing them is by means of suggestive pictures of tasteful scenes associated with the article, or by a tempting array of pictures of the objects themselves, in a setting which itself possesses agreeable feeling tone.

The important thing here is the necessity of avoiding *disagreeable images* or *negative suggestions,* either in,

PRINCIPLES OF APPEAL AND RESPONSE

1. The picture itself.
2. The reading matter.
3. The name or brand mark.
4. The adjacent advertisements.
5. Chance associations.

These points can be best illustrated by giving instances of their violation.

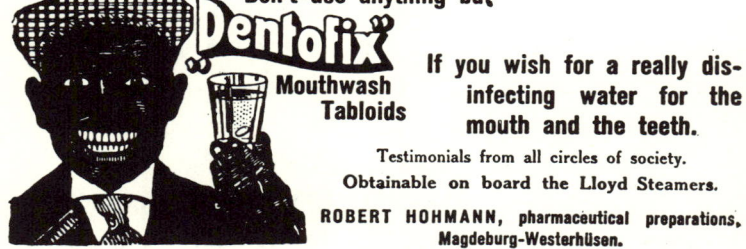

INAPPROPRIATE FEELING TONE MAY IN SOME CASES BE PROVOKED BY THIS ADVERTISEMENT

1. The picture of a guest at a restaurant table refusing a substitute for some article the name of which appears nearby in bold type is likely to associate the act of rejection with the very article advertised.

2. The suggestions of substitutes, even in the nature of warning, is considered in general to be a bad method psychologically. It calls up extrinsic, foreign imagery, in the place of relevant pictures.

FEELING TONE OF CONTENT

3. The third point is constantly violated by advertisements which associate disagreeable words, objects or people with the commodity, as

> Slimy fish with medicine
> Guinea pigs with toilet preparations
> Tramps with soap and lotions
> Cattle with tobacco
> Frogs with coffee
> A dirty floor with soup
> Butterflies with sugar etc.

FEELING TONE OF ASSOCIATIONS INAPPROPRIATELY USED. Cover of a folder issued by Schonland Bros., sausage manufacturers in Portland, Me. (From *Advertising and Selling*, Dec., 1910.)

4. Writers have frequently pointed out the futility of placing a breakfast food advertisement alongside one for an asthma cure, that of a delicate dessert next to a remedy for eczema, etc. The important principle here is that the feeling tone of an appeal depends not entirely on our reaction to that appeal alone, but also on our

general mood at the time. And this general mood is easily influenced by adjacent advertisements, recent experiences, etc.

5. In illustration of the rôle of chance associations we may instance two facts:

A. An article may be surrounded with a favorable atmosphere, a favorable association cluster, by utilizing an atmosphere already created for another purpose. Thus our attitude toward a Yale bicycle or a Yale pipe is influenced by what we already know of the efficiency of Yale locks or of the prowess and reliability of Yale's football team. Arcadia Mixture smoking tobacco has been sold to many a smoker because of the delightful atmosphere previously drawn about the name in J. M. Barrie's "My Lady Nicotine." There may be certain unethical features involved in such utilization of borrowed atmosphere, but the psychological basis for its success remains, nevertheless.

B. Synæsthesia.—An interesting phenomenon which may some day become of concrete use to the advertisement writer is the fact that certain sensations are often closely associated with sensations from quite different sense departments. Thus sounds of musical instruments, vowels, syllables, may be seen to be *colored*. One man on

FEELING TONE OF CONTENT

record sees consonants as purplish black, while the vowels vary in color. "U" is a light dove color, "e" is pale emerald, "a" is yellow, etc. Thinking of the word "Tuesday," the first part seems light gray-green and the latter part yellow.

In some cases colors accompany the sensations of taste and smell. Salt, for instance, is described by one observer as dull red, bitter as brown, sour as green or greenish-blue, and sweet as clear bright red. One observer sees the taste of meat as red and brown, Graham bread as a rich red, and all ice creams—except chocolate and coffee—as blue. To another observer the sound of the word "intelligence" tastes like fresh sliced tomatoes and "interest" like stewed tomatoes!

These synæsthesias, as they are called, seem, however, to be so individual and personal that no two people are likely to agree on them by present methods of inquiry. If there were more general laws there could be much clever and subtle selection of appropriate colors, words, etc. At present, however, no such laws can be announced.

STRAIN AND RELAXATION

In discussing the suggestive character of horizontal and diagonal lines we have already had

PRINCIPLES OF APPEAL AND RESPONSE

occasion to refer to *feelings of strain and relaxation*. Feelings of this sort are of particular importance in another connection, that of the legibility of type when an appeal is presented to the sense of sight. Many an advertisement fails to

---

THE HOTEL SEVILLE OFFERS VERY DESIRABLE SUITES OF ANY NUMBER OF ROOMS, WITH ALL MODERN IMPROVEMENTS. THE ROOMS ARE OF VARIOUS SIZES, EQUIPPED WITH LARGE CLOSETS, ARE WELL FURNISHED AND WELL ARRANGED. THE TABLE (A LA CARTE) AND ITS APPOINTMENTS ARE STRICTLY FIRST CLASS. WELL-TRAINED WHITE SERVANTS RENDER STRICTLY UP-TO-DATE SERVICE. ROOMS AND SUITES ARE RENTED BY THE DAY, BY THE SEASON AND BY THE YEAR. A VERY QUIET YET CENTRAL LOCATION, APPEALING PARTICULARLY TO PEOPLE OF REFINEMENT

MADISON AVENUE AND
TWENTY-NINTH STREET.

EDW. PURCHAS,
MANAGER.

STRAIN

influence simply because it is so difficult to read that few individuals take the pains to decipher it. The Hotel Seville announcement shows an advertisement of this sort, which has caught my eye many times, but which to this day I have not yet read, nor shall I ever read it through. Compare this hotel announcement with that of the Bel-

FEELING TONE OF CONTENT

nord. The comfortable legibility of the latter contrasts strongly with the hopelessness of the former. The former is an example of strain, the

---

⁋The BELNORD is built in the form of a hollow square, enclosing the largest apartment house court in existence. Every room is an outside room. Each suite, 7 to 11 rooms, includes numerous modern devices for extra comfort and convenience.

⁋The absence of noise and vibration has been achieved by locating the engine rooms under the central court and not under any part of the building proper. Yearly rentals begin at $2,400.

⁋A visit to the BELNORD will save you many fatiguing days of "apartment hunting." Interested parties are cordially invited.

W. H. DOLSON & CO., Agents

Office on the Premises

2364 Broadway, at 86th St.   *Telephone 10400—River.*

RELAXATION

latter an example of relaxation, both being dependent on the legibility of the appeal. In this connection it may be useful to point out some of the factors which make for legibility of printed matter.

PRINCIPLES OF APPEAL AND RESPONSE

1. *Favorable Length of Printed Lines.*—Experimental studies of the way in which the eye behaves in reading show that the whole line of

THE USE OF LOWER CASE LETTERS AND OF FAVORABLE LENGTH OF LINE. Reading matter made legible and more likely both to attract and to hold the reader's attention.

printed matter is not seen at once and as a whole by the eye. Nor are the separate letters each fixated in succession, nor are the successive words even examined one by one. The eye fixates three or four points in reading the line, these points falling where they may—now in the middle of a word, now at the beginning or end, now between two words. When the printing is legible a given line thus requires few movements for the comprehension of the words—a few fixations will cover the whole of the line. But when the printing is difficult to read clearly, the separate letters or words difficult to discriminate from each other, more fixations are required, and these extra fixations mean strain and fatigue. The most comfortable length of line, for ordinary printing, is found to be about three and one-half inches.

2. *Appropriate Spacing of Letters, Words and Lines.*—The spacing used should indicate the natural unities of the material presented. Thus the space between letters making up a word should be less than the width of the letters themselves, while the space between adjacent words should be greater than either of these two distances. The space between sentences should be somewhat greater still. If a number of lines are intended to belong together as a unit or paragraph, the spacing between the various lines should be somewhat less than the width of the lines themselves (as measured by the height of the letters). If this rule is not followed, the space

PRINCIPLES OF APPEAL AND RESPONSE

between paragraphs should be then increased, in order to suggest the unity of the **paragraphs**. In-

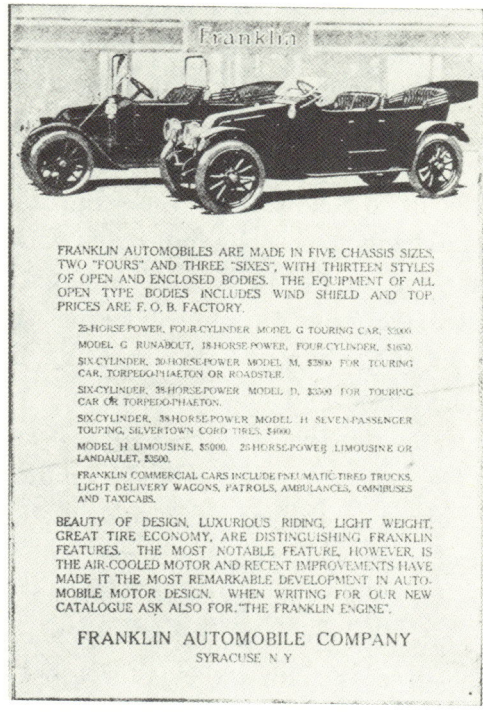

ILLEGIBILITY RESULTING FROM THE EXCLUSIVE USE OF CAPITAL LETTERS IN READING MATTER DESIGNED TO HOLD THE READER'S ATTENTION.

dentation of paragraphs and even of every other line in the printed matter is found to facilitate the process of reading.

3. We have already seen that we tend to find

FEELING TONE OF CONTENT

meaning in the tops rather than in the bases of things. This is particularly true in reading

ILLEGIBILITY AND STRAIN ARE PRODUCED BY TOO GREAT VARIETY OF TYPE FACES, INTERRUPTED LINES AND INEFFECTIVE SPACING. All of these make rhythmical movements and adjustments impossible.

printed matter. The eye tends to follow the upper part of the line of letters, and the upper parts of the type faces are the parts which show variety and differentiation as between the different let-

PRINCIPLES OF APPEAL AND RESPONSE

ters. Partly for this reason the "lower case" letters are more easily perceived and read than are

ILLUSTRATING THE EASE OF READING AND FEELING OF RELAXATION PRODUCED BY THE USE OF LOWER CASE LETTERS AND BY THE PRESENCE OF APPROPRIATE SPACING.

capital letters. Franklin Automobile Company's advertisement illustrates the difficulty of reading printed matter composed entirely of capitals. In the case of the Peck-Williamson Company's advertisement the illegibility is also partly a matter of faulty spacing. The Baldwin Company's advertisement combines the ease of "lower case" letters with favorable and appropriate spacing. It also shows the ease with which the "lower case" letters are read.

4. Ease of reading is interfered with by too great a variety of type faces. Thus the "Underfeed" advertisement is most illegible, partly because of the lack of unity and organization, but largely also because the thirty different kinds of letters and type faces occurring on a single page call for excessive and uncomfortable changes in adjustment at irregular intervals. One of the things which most facilitates easy reading is the possibility of falling into rhythmical habits of eye movement across the page and back again, and rhythmical changes of adjustment of the optical apparatus from moment to moment.

5. A fifth factor of importance is the fact that not all type faces of the same size are equally legible. The type faces which happen to have been most used in printed advertisements turn out, under experimental conditions, to be the least legible of a large group of faces and styles which were studied. The table on page 187 gives the legibility of each of nine different faces, lower

case letters only, when these letters occur grouped as in words. The legibility was measured by determining the maximum distance, in daylight illumination, at which the letters could be correctly identified. Each letter of the alphabet was tested 12 times, twice by each of 6 observers, and the results of the 26 letters were averaged to give the final measure of the type face as a whole. The measures in the table give the number of centimeters at which the given type face can, on the average, be read. All letters used were what are known as 10 point letters, the faces all being Roman, no bold or italic faces being used. Tables for upper case letters and for lower case letters, for 16 different faces, the letters occurring both in groups and in isolation, may be found in an article by Roethlein in the *American Journal of Psychology* of January, 1912. Legibility was found to vary little with the form of the type, but to depend chiefly on the size, width of line, and amount of white space exposed between the letters. The faces differ less when the letters are grouped than they do when the letters are observed in isolation. And it must be said here that even these measurements are by no means complete statements of the legibility of the type faces when used in printing, because much of our reading is done, not by perceiving the separate letters which make up the words, but very largely by recognizing the words as wholes, by means of their characteristic "word forms."

Type Face	Order of Legibility, cm. distance
News Gothic	166
Cushing Old Style	165
Century Old Style	162
Cheltenham Wide	159
Century Expanded	159
Scotch Roman	151
Bullfinch	150
Caslon	149
Cushing Monotype	144

Illustrations of these faces may be found in many manuals of reference and data books used by printers and advertising men.

6. A final factor which may be mentioned as contributing toward relaxation in reading printed matter is the background on which the letters occur. A maximum brightness difference between background and type makes for easy perception. When colored background or type is used, the same rule holds, for it is not the difference in color as such, but the difference in the brightness values of the colors used which is effective. We have already had occasion, when discussing *contrast* as an attention device, to explain the greater attention value of black on white, as contrasted with white on black, and to point out that we are

not concerned there with a real difference in legibility. There is some difficulty in reading printed matter which does not differ sufficiently from the brightness of the background on which it appears.

CHAPTER XI

THE THIRD TASK: FIXING THE IMPRESSION

Clearly the work of an appeal does not stop with attracting attention or even with holding it until the copy is read. Rival appeals will be operating, and, if they are at all effective, will have a certain persistence in the consciousness of the reader. Evidently an essential function is that of being able to so impress the reader that in a later moment, when there is *need* felt for an article of the general type, this particular brand will suggest itself as the first of its kind. This recurrence of a previous idea we call a recollection. Now, ideas do not spring up spontaneously in the mind. So far as we can see, an idea is always introduced by virtue of its connection with a preceding thought. If in a moment of need the specific name of an article designated to fill that need is thought of, this happens because that particular name has been, as we say, associated, linked up with the situation of need more firmly than any other name for a similar article. This dominance of ideas is what we are concerned with in the psychology of *association*. Ideas occur by virtue of previous connections, and these connections are determined by definite laws, can be brought about and facilitated by specific devices, or weakened by failure to conform to these rules.

We shall be better able to understand the laws of association by knowing something of the nervous processes on which they depend. Association takes place when nervous energy from one center flows out into related centers, causing a corresponding related consciousness. This overflowing of energy must take place along a nervous pathway, and this pathway must be formed in the nervous tissue before the exchange is direct. The general rule is that energy radiates out in all directions from a center so long as all the possible paths have equal resistance. Now, if two adjacent centers should discharge at the same moment, there would be a pathway between them which would be doubly excited, and hence its resistance would be lowered. Thus suppose three processes, A, B, C, to have occurred at the same time. Such a pathway will be at once formed between the centers corresponding to these processes. Whenever either of the three occurs at a

FIXING THE IMPRESSION

later moment it will tend to excite the centers corresponding to each of the others. *Every element thus tends to bring up again the whole of which it was previously a part.* Thus the sight of either of the three words, "Company," "Boston" or "Rubber" will tend to remind the reader of the whole phrase, "Boston Rubber Company."

Three primary laws may be laid down here:

1. Every nervous current leaves traces of its pathway.
2. This trace facilitates the passage of subsequent impulses over the same pathway.
3. Such a pathway tends to drain off energy from other centers which may be active only in a random way.

This process of linkage between the two ideas such as "Boston" and "Rubber" is what we mean by *association*.

PRINCIPLES OF CONNECTION

There are two fundamental principles of association which advertisements persistently and flagrantly violate. In natural thinking there are two laws that control the play of our ideas. Both laws are true in general. But in order for the

PRINCIPLES OF APPEAL AND RESPONSE

advertiser to be effective, he must set one of these laws against the other.

1. The first law is that *we tend habitually to think from particular to general*. If I hear or read "Ingersoll" I at once think "watch," the general class of which the "Ingersoll" is but a particular. If I hear "Rambler" I think "bicycle," "Ditson"—"saws," "Maydole"—"hammers," etc. Now, this is a perfectly natural tendency, but it is of no use to the advertiser, who wants us, not so much to think "watch" when we hear "Ingersoll," as to think "Ingersoll" when we need a watch, "Cluett" when we need a shirt, "Burns" when the general idea "coal" is in the mind. That is, in order to attain his end, the advertiser must force us to *violate a fundamental law of thinking* and to go not from "shirt" to its class "garment," but down to a *particular* shirt as "Cluett."

Now, the strangest part of it all is that the average advertisement not only fails to realize this necessity, but even works against itself by failing to recognize the second general law, *the forward law*.

2. *We tend to think forward rather than backward*. Associations tend to take their original direction and have only little influence in the

FIXING THE IMPRESSION

reverse direction. You cannot tell me without some reflection what letter comes before the letter "I" in our alphabet. When you can, you will find that you have recalled it by starting with "A" and going *forward*. From "H" to "I" is a perfectly natural transition, but from "I" to "H" is a violation of the law. Similarly you can tell me much more quickly last names of men with given first names than you can the first names of a row of last names. The same is true with a line of poetry. The first word calls up the whole line, but the last word, although it has previously existed in consciousness along with the preceding words, does not tend to call them up to anything like the same degree. Subsequent impulses tend not only to follow old pathways, but they tend to follow them in the direction of the original connection. So if I hear "George" I tend at once to think "Washington." But if I hear "Washington," I do not go back to "George," but forward to "monument," "square," "bridge," etc.

The reason for this first principle is simply that nervous energy tends to spread out from the centers of origin into all related or connected centers, thus calling into play the whole class. The reason for the second law is not clear, but we

PRINCIPLES OF APPEAL AND RESPONSE

may be sure that it has some stable basis in the structure of the nervous pathways.

Here, then, we have a principle which can be employed to counteract the tendency of **principle 1**.

FORWARD REASONING—CORRECT ARRANGEMENT

We tend to think from particular to general, *other things being equal*. But, if in reading an advertisement, our thought has been repeatedly led from a general to a given particular, by the composer putting the general term first and following it by the particular, *the second law is able*

FIXING THE IMPRESSION

to offset the first. The general rule should be, then:

BACKWARD REASONING—INCORRECT ARRANGEMENT. **The effective method is to *present first* the name of the commodity, or the idea, need, occasion, which shall be in the reader's mind on subsequent occasions. *Follow this* by the name of the particular brand, the firm name, the trade mark, the slogan, etc., which you desire him to think of at the moment when he thinks of the commodity or feels the particular need.**

Place first the *general class,* the *purpose or use* to which the article can be put, the word which will be in consciousness *in the moment of **need***. Thus, "the best of Christmas gifts."

Place next the *name of the article or brand* which you desire to connect with the need, or which you desire to make the standard specimen for the general class in question. See the Copley prints advertisements.

If, instead, the first word in the advertisement were "Copley prints," and only later came the words, "best Christmas gift," the idea of "prints" would come to remind the reader of "Christmas," but when he found himself thinking over the "best gift" to purchase there would be no particularly strong inclination to think of "Copley prints."

It seems to the writer that no law is violated oftener than this in current advertising, and that the law is no mere subtlety but an important element in the general efficiency of copy. In fact, the law may be conformed to so fully that the specific brand may come to be synonymous, in the mind of the public, with the general class or use. When this point is reached it becomes necessary to teach not association but dissociation. Thus the Kodak copy must now teach people that not all cameras are Kodaks. The law of association worked so thoroughly here that it now operates

FIXING THE IMPRESSION

against its original purpose. The case nicely illustrates the fallacy of relying solely on any one principle and disregarding others.

The chief method of fixing an impression received from an advertisement is by connecting it up with the stimulus in which the need for some such article will be felt. There are various ways in which this connection may be made.

I. LAWS OF ORIGINAL CONNECTION

1. *Contiguity.*—This is perhaps the most frequent cause of association. Things perceived side by side, either in space or time, tend to suggest each other, on recurrence of either. Thus "Brooklyn Bridge" calls up "East River."

If a place of business is announced as being "one block from Grand Central" or "near Herald Square," the thought or sight of Grand Central or Herald Square will tend to revive, by association, the name, business, and location of the advertised store.

2. *Similarity.*—Things bearing a resemblance to each other tend to call each other up in consciousness. They do this because certain elements in the two facts are identical, hence tend to call up both wholes of which they have previ-

ously been a part. Thus one person reminds one of another because the two have identically shaped noses. One biscuit reminds one of another because the color of the box is the same. The Jungfrau reminds us of Pike's Peak; Moxine reminds us of Moxie, and will take unto itself any atmosphere of desirability that Moxie has developed. Similarly Yale locks will sell Yale bicycles. The general sentiment seems to be against the use of such similarity appeal as is involved in the reference to substitutes and imitations. Obviously this is only from the point of view of the original article. If you happen to be engaged in the manufacture of substitutes the more of the original atmosphere you can borrow, the better.

3. *The third basis of association is emotional congruity.* This simply means that the *feelings* aroused by two different experiences are the same, and whenever one comes, the feeling produced tends to call up the other also. Thus falling from a trapeze once reminded me vividly of a time when I was chased by an Indian with a tomahawk. The importance of the æsthetic factors of an advertisement comes here strongly into prominence. Not only do pleasing advertisements attract us, and hold us, but we in turn hold them.

FIXING THE IMPRESSION

Furthermore, any experience with strong feeling tone is better retained than indifferent facts. This is of especial importance in appeals over the short circuit, appeals to feelings and emotions for the sake of vividness.

Connection with pleasurable emotions fixates associations and tends to lead to action. Appeals through sympathy, loyalty, interest, civic pride, local atmosphere, through excitement over current events, through prevalent ideas, crazes, desires, movements, etc., will all tend to be more or less successful, though transiently so. Such advertising must keep constantly changing in tone and direction, and it is both difficult and expensive to "keep one's finger on the public pulse" closely and delicately enough to be able to use these social currents to advantage. When the local excitement has blown over and the incident tends to be forgotten, the article advertised in connection with it tends to be forgotten along with it.

A safer plan is to utilize the stable and permanent emotions more or less common to all times and places. Thus a powerful basis of appeal and spring of conduct, for certain kinds of commodities, is the religious emotion. It is reported that a book entitled "Wonders of Nature" fell flat on the market. The title was changed to "Wonders of Nature and Architecture of God,'' and a second edition was at once called for.

II. PRINCIPLES OF REVIVAL

The foregoing are called the *principles of connection* because they have to do with the process by which an association is originally produced. But the fact that a connection has been made does not guarantee the reproduction of the pair. For several ideas might each have been connected with the stimulus, and they could not all be revived at once. There is, then, a further question, viz., how, granted a connection once made, can we be sure that one associate will come rather than some other?

In answer to this question we find a group of principles which we may call the *principles of revival* as distinguished from the *principles of connection*. The first four are the most important. They are, in order of their relative strength:

1. *Frequency.*—Other things being equal, the association most often repeated will be the strongest connection. ''Theodore'' suggests ''Roosevelt,'' rather than ''Sturm,'' ''Cousins,'' or any other associate, simply because it has occurred more frequently than any other. Every repeti-

FIXING THE IMPRESSION

tion strengthens the connection, just as every rabbit hopping through the snow emphasizes and defines the path of the rabbit which passed that way before. This is the principle of repetition in advertising. Repetition has both a memory and response value, as we shall see later. In experiments in the laboratory, counting "normal association," or that which results after unemphasized reading, as 26 per cent., *repetition* gives an average value of 64 per cent., nearly three times the memory value of unrepeated material. So among practical men, repetition is considered an effective, albeit an expensive, method of securing publicity. As we have already seen, different kinds of material vary somewhat with respect to their attention value in repetition, relevant words increasing, all cuts decreasing, and irrelevant words remaining on a level. But so far as memory goes, repetition, *if supported by attention,* always strengthens the impression.

2. *The second factor* in relative strength is *vividness.* Vividness may be brought about in many ways—through sheer intensity, through surprise, strong attention, interest, or through connection with some emotion, as fear, hope, envy, etc. The more vivid the impression, the longer it lasts. Strong colors, enormous signs, humor-

PRINCIPLES OF APPEAL AND RESPONSE

ous associations, motor responses such as clipping a coupon, sending an inquiry, etc., are merely varied ways of producing vividness. Compared with the normal value, 26 per cent., vividness gives an experimental average of 52 per cent. efficiency.

Closely related to vividness, and being, perhaps, only special forms of it are:

3. *Recency,* with an average value of 50 per cent., and

4. *Primacy,* with a value of 46 per cent.

When all other factors are equal, we can be sure that the first association will predominate. At least the first and last impressions have the advantage. We have already discussed this in the section on "position."

The Curve of Forgetting.—Another important point has to do with the most effective distribution of a series of appeals which are to be addressed, one after the other, to the same person. Circulars, follow-up literature, educational campaigns, etc., often afford instances of this method of appeal. The ordinary method is to distribute the successive appeals according to the calendar divisions of time, as every week or ten days, every two weeks, etc., until all the appeals have been presented. This method proceeds on the as-

FIXING THE IMPRESSION

sumption that the reader's memory and interest are controlled by the movements of the celestial or terrestrial bodies, while the fact is that memory follows laws of its own, regardless of the conventional and calendar divisions of the passage of time. When a given appeal is addressed to me, I straightway proceed to forget it. But I do not forget it at a uniform rate, so much being forgotten on each succeeding day until all is forgot-

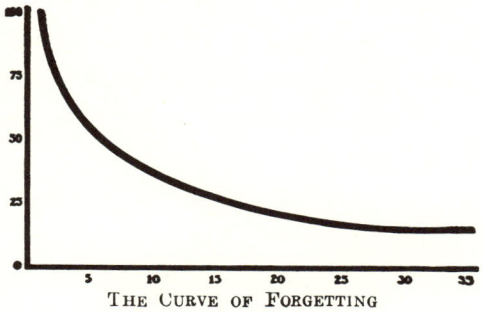

THE CURVE OF FORGETTING

ten. Instead I forget the material that has been seen or learned, according to a definite "curve of forgetting," a curve which descends rapidly at first and then more slowly. The larger proportion of the material is forgotten in the first day or so. After that a constantly decreasing amount is forgotten on each succeeding day.

The height of the curve above the base line here indicates the amount remembered, the figures

PRINCIPLES OF APPEAL AND RESPONSE

along the base indicating the units of time elapsed since first learning the material. During the first ten units as much is forgotten as during all the remaining twenty-five. Of course, the amounts and time units in the accompanying curve are purely arbitrary. Their real value will depend on the quality and the quantity of the material learned and on the time interval chosen. But the form of the curve shows clearly that by far the greater number of repetitions should come at the beginning of the campaign, when the tendency to forget is strong. When the maximum of retention is then reached the later repetitions may be farther and farther apart.

It ought to be obvious at once that the effective distribution of a series of appeals will be a distribution which conforms to this curve of forgetting. The first appeal having been presented, the second should follow close upon it, the third at a somewhat greater interval from the second, the fourth a somewhat longer time after the third, etc., the intervals growing longer and longer until the series is completed. This massing of the appeals at the earlier portion of the total period will result in reinforcement of the first appeal at the crucial moments, the moments when, unless thus reinforced, they tend to be quickly forgot-

FIXING THE IMPRESSION

ten, thus leaving the later appeals to appear on what is practically barren ground. That is to say, the effective distribution of a series of appeals addressed to the same person will not follow a calendar order such as the following:

1	2	3	4	5
Initial Appeal	After One Week	After Two Weeks	After Three Weeks	After Four Weeks

but will follow a distribution based on the curve of forgetting, as:

1	2	3	4	5
Initial Appeal	After 2 Days	After 5 Days	After 10 Days	After 20 Days

Any one may convince himself of the existence of this law by simply trying to memorize a given amount of material of any sort, by distributing his learning periods or repetitions according to the two plans. This law seems to me to be one of the most important results of the experimental study of memory, and one which the practical man has been surprisingly slow in appropriating.

MINOR DEVICES

Further minor devices for aiding the memory value are: *Ingenuity, rhyme, rhythm,* and *motor reinforcement.* These are really nothing more than forms of vividness, but are distinct enough from each other to merit separate mention.

PRINCIPLES OF APPEAL AND RESPONSE

1. *Ingenuity.*—Just as *novelty* attracts attention and holds it, a curious, bizarre name, package, trade mark is likely to stick. Such words as "Uneeda Biscuit," "Keen Kutter," "Rough on Rats," "Ever Stick," "No Smellee," stick in one's consciousness. The merchant with

> Street No. 33
> Telephone No. 33
> Letters in name, 33
> Price of suit, $33

could easily make up an ingenious and impressive advertisement (see Scott). But to be effective under this heading a name must be really ingenious, not merely a hybrid.

2. *Rhyme* and *alliteration* are other things that attract attention and are easily remembered because they suggest in themselves a single unified scheme on which to hang the separate facts.

3. Closely related also is *rhythm,* which reduces the learning of a given amount of material about 40-50 per cent., by lending motor control and further means of association with movements. The writer once tried to teach the English alphabet to a kindergarten class of German children. Several days' effort was unsuccessful. At last the idea occurred to set the letters to the tune of

FIXING THE IMPRESSION

"Yankee Doodle" and sing them with the class. The alphabet was learned in a single recitation period. Similarly the names of things sung in rhythm or rhyme on the advertising cards tend to be retained. This does not mean, however, that the goods thus sung will necessarily be sold. It is one thing to make a commodity known as "worthy of song" and quite another thing to make it known as "worth buying."

4. *Motor reinforcement* is one of the important aids to memory. Try to memorize a verse of poetry. You will at once find yourself making sets of movements which are designed to aid you in retaining the material; you speak the words to yourself, moving the lips meanwhile, or you write the lines on paper or accompany the learning process by tapping the toes, swinging the body to and fro, nodding the head, etc. Just as clenching the fist or gripping a piece of wood reinforces the leap or brace which one is about to give, so the performance of a motor process in connection with an idea tends strongly to impress that idea in memory. You remember the thing you have done yourself much more easily than the things you have passively observed others performing—the words you write much more easily than the sentence you merely read.

PRINCIPLES OF APPEAL AND RESPONSE

Herein lies the chief importance of invitations to clip out the advertisement, to draw the figure, to write for information or catalogues, to tear off and preserve or return coupons, etc. If the reader can be induced to carry out any such action in connection with the advertisement, the memory value of the copy will be tremendously enhanced. And this follows, not only because more time is spent on the advertisement and more thought given to it, but largely because the motor response reinforces the mental impression.

Obviously the success of such devices will usually depend on the ease with which the action can be carried out. The ideal would be the longest act which the average reader would carry out without the sense of lost time.

MEMORABILITY OF DIFFERENT KINDS OF FACTS

An important factor in putting an article on the market or in keeping it there is that of having a trade mark, emblem, seal, design, or name, by which the article may always be remembered, asked for, recognized and recommended. Herein enter in large measure the preceding factors of rhyme, rhythm, alliteration and ingenuity. But another highly important factor which is little recognized is that of the *memorability of different*

FIXING THE IMPRESSION

kinds of material. In selecting a mark by which goods, designed for popular consumption, are to be known, it is of real value, for instance, to know that *persons* and *faces* are more easily remembered than *objects,* and *objects* more easily than *actions;* that *form* is more easily remembered and recognized than *color,* although *colors* are more accurately remembered than *numbers.* More numbers can be remembered than colors, but they are likely to be wrongly remembered or remembered as existing in a false order or position.

In a carefully conducted experiment in the writer's laboratory the investigator measured the accuracy with which 40 persons in an audience could observe and remember for a period of three days the various features of an elaborately planned performance which was carried on in their presence. The reliability of each witness was measured, along with the accuracy with which different sorts of facts were reported.

The individual reliability ranged from 38 per cent. to 82 per cent. accuracy, with an average of 62 per cent. It is important to note, then, that the ordinary witness observes only about 60 per cent. of the features of an event to which his attention is already directed. That is to say, 40 per cent. of the advertisements and 40 per cent.

PRINCIPLES OF APPEAL AND RESPONSE

of each advertisement will, on the average, pass unnoticed. Moreover, only about 2 per cent. of readers normally see advertisements. (See Strong.) This gives 2 per cent. of 60 = about 1 per cent. efficiency. Which features, then, will most likely be observed and retained correctly?

The table for this experiment, indicating the relative accuracy with which different sorts of facts are reported when direct questions are asked concerning them, runs as follows:

TABLE X

		Accuracy
1.	Mere presence of things	97%
2.	Number of people	65%
3.	Space relations, form, etc.	58%
4.	Condition of objects	48%
5.	Order of events	35%
6.	Color	26%
7.	Size and quantity	22%
8.	Sounds	10%
9.	Time (duration)	8%
10.	Actions (strong attention value but not accurately reported)	

The importance of these facts in selecting trade marks, packages, names, slogans, and points of emphasis for advertising purposes is constantly disregarded.

Another experiment was designed to measure the relative memory value of cuts as compared with that of reading matter. For this experi-

FIXING THE IMPRESSION

ment proof slips of advertisements designed and kindly furnished by Will Phillip Hooper were used. The advertisements were uniform in size and style, and all contained about equal amounts of cut and reading matter. Twenty-five of these advertisements were examined by each of the observers, who were then requested to select from a collection of ninety advertisements those which they had previously seen. Of the twenty-five original cards, fifteen were present unchanged. Of the remaining ten, five contained the same cut, but the text had been changed, while five retained the original text but bore a totally new cut. The idea was to discover which of these two changes, of cut or of text, would attract more attention, and which would most disturb the memory of the observer.

The following table resulted, showing: (1) that the change in the cut is most frequently detected, thus that the cut has greater *attention* value; (2) that cards with changed cuts are remembered by the text more often than cards with changed text are remembered by the cut, that is that the *memory* value of text is higher than that of cuts; (3) that the combination of the original cut with original text has much higher memory

PRINCIPLES OF APPEAL AND RESPONSE

value than that of either of the two mutilated forms.

TABLE XI

Normal ads recognized	77%
Ads with right text but wrong cut	56%
Ads with right cut but wrong text	43%
Substitution of cut detected	26%
Substitution of text detected	17%

TRADE MARKS

In the same laboratory a study has been made of the relative attention and memory value of different geometric forms, such as are commonly used as trade marks. Fifty such designs were chosen, of the same general size and same color. Experiments on twenty-five observers showed these forms to differ widely in the respect tested. The values range from 28 per cent. to 92 per cent. The following plate gives the list of these forms and also the percentage of accuracy with which each was recognized when a group of fifteen previously displayed was selected from a set of fifty which included the original fifteen and thirty-five strange forms. The general principle suggested by this experiment is that those forms are best remembered to which specific names can be given, as "star," "crescent," "crown," etc.

FIXING THE IMPRESSION

RELATIVE ATTENTION VALUE OF 50 GEOMETRICAL FORMS

VICARIOUS SACRIFICES IN ADVERTISING

The failure to observe the foregoing laws of association and memory often leads to what may be called "vicarious sacrifice" in advertising. A century ago we could consume faster than we could produce. The situation now is frequently said to be just the reverse, the advertiser often finding it necessary to stimulate consumption. He finds it necessary to create a new need, or to invest an old need with greater urgency, just as Hand Sapolio tried to create an ideal of cleanliness among people not using soap, or as Sapolio created a higher ideal of cleanliness of pots and kettles. (See Balmer, p. 34.)

Once such a demand is created, *non-advertised* articles at once share in the profits. In so far as this happens, the work of the advertiser may be said to be vicarious; it is a free will offering to the non-advertiser. Such sacrifice, however, is often due to the advertising. Thus the early Subway cards of Boston Rubber Company with their "Wet Feet Did It" warnings certainly created a greater demand for *rubbers in general,* but *not* for Boston Rubbers in particular, because this particular brand was not carefully associated in the mind of the reader with the *need.* Experiments which the writer was making with a set of seventy-five subway advertisements at the time showed clearly the tendency not to notice the brand advertised on these cards at all, but to connect the warnings and general feelings of need with a striking card advertising the "Ever Stick"

FIXING THE IMPRESSION

rubber, which, so far as the writer's knowledge goes, was a rival product. Since that time these cards have been greatly improved.

In conclusion, we may say that a successful advertisement not only *attracts* and *holds attention,* but in so doing it *connects a specific brand or article with a general need,* so that when the general need is felt, the action will not be toward such articles in general, but toward this specific brand in particular. In the following chapter on *provoking the response* we shall seek to analyze still further the ways in which this specific action may be brought about.

CHAPTER XII

THE FOURTH TASK: PROVOKING THE RESPONSE

After all has been said, the final value of an appeal depends entirely upon the effectiveness with which it leads to the desired specific action. No amount of care in framing a solicitation so as to catch the eye, to hold attention, and to stick in the memory, will be worth the trouble if the reader's reaction does not go beyond the appeal itself, and include the article which the appeal announces. Granted, then, that the first three tasks have been adequately performed, what are the principles which control the direction, the certainty, and the force of the response?

Obviously there are two cases to be considered here. First, the case in which the appeal is addressed directly to the life of feeling, impulse and instinct—what we have called the *short-circuit appeal*—and, second, the case in which deliberation, comparison and argument are invited— the "reason why" appeal by means of the *long circuit*. In the first case there is no conflict or rivalry stirred up in the reader's consciousness; there is simply the attempt to present the article in such a way as to provoke some firmly grounded act of appropriation, to stir up some strong impulse or keen desire and so to lead to favorable action. In the second type conflict is, on the contrary, even encouraged. Selling points, superiorities, advantages, etc., are advanced, and the claims of rival commodities deliberately challenged.

It will be difficult to speak in terms of general laws here, and yet to remain concrete. Conditions will vary according to the article, the reader's temperament and need, local influences, habits and customs. The result is that this is one of the most promising fields for further research in applied and practical psychology. Some of the experiments that are already in progress in the field of advertising will be reported in the chapter on the experimental method. But there is a certain group of principles which can be clearly stated and applied on the basis of what we already know of mental processes in the life of action. These we will take up in turn. Our chief concern will be with the laws of suggestion and with our earlier question concerning the appropriate use of long and short circuit appeals.

PRINCIPLES OF APPEAL AND RESPONSE

DIRECT APPEALS TO FEELING

Short Circuit Action Without Conflict.—We may distinguish two general types of short circuit appeal:

(a) The appeal through command, assertion, invitation, either direct or indirect. Such an appeal will owe its force to the degree to which it conforms to the *laws of suggestion.* At this point, then, these *laws of suggestion* must come in for their share of discussion.

(b) The second type will be the appeal to some definite instinct, or other strong and certain form of reaction. Success here will depend chiefly on the strength and promptness of the instinct to which the appeal is made. Here, then, will be the place to consider the topic to which we have so frequently referred, but as often postponed for later discussion, viz., the question of the relative strength of the various human instincts, and their dependence on such factors as age, sex, class, occupation, training, the commodity in question, etc.

THE NATURE AND LAWS OF SUGGESTION

No little mystery has come to invest the word "suggestion," chiefly because of its constant use

PROVOKING THE RESPONSE

by pseudo-scientific writers in their attempts to develop dramatic interest in the extreme suggestibility of certain states of drowsiness, abstraction, fatigue and hysteria. But there is no more mystery here than there is in any of the simple mental processes along the nervous arc. The fundamental law is that of *ideo-motor action*.[1] In the earlier discussion of the nervous basis of mental processes, we pointed out the law that *every sensory impulse has its inevitable motor issue*. The nervous energy generated or liberated by a stimulus emerges at the other end of the arc in the form of action. This action is usually directed toward the stimulus itself, in the form of movements of appropriation or rejection. Sometimes, however, the response is not so apparent, when, for instance, it takes the form of general bodily attitude, changes in breathing, heart beat, gland action, vascular changes, or general rigidity or tension of muscles. Moreover, the strength of the reaction need not be exactly proportionate to the strength of the stimulus. Sometimes the energy may be drained off into other channels that are active at the time,

---

[1] The psychological reader should not confuse the law of ideo-motor action, as here presented, with the doctrine that the cause of a voluntary movement is a kinæsthetic image of that movement.

and the value of the response will then be obscured. Again, the direct response may itself drain off energy from other pathways, and its strength be relatively increased.

Closely connected with this law of the inevitable motor issue of sensory impulses is a correlate law which concerns mental processes that do not have an immediate sensory cause. In the section on Imagination we have seen that we may have ideas and images even when there is no corresponding activity of the sense organ. These processes are then due to what we may call the spontaneous activity of the brain centers. This spontaneity, however, will only mean independence of a *corresponding* sensory impression. But the activity will usually be seen to be caused by virtue of the association of the center in question with some other center whose previous activity has stirred it up in what seems to be a spontaneous way. Often the activity is due to some present sensory impression, which, however, does not *correspond* in character to that of the spontaneous image or idea. Frequently this impression is simply a word—the auditory impression of syllables spoken or the visual impression of a written or printed word. The word center is closely associated with the sensory center which

PROVOKING THE RESPONSE

is involved when we actually perceive the object which the word denotes or means. Hence, activity from the word center overflows into the object center, and the result is an apparently spontaneous image, picture, or idea of the object or act which the word suggests.

Now these so-called spontaneous nervous processes have their tendency to motor issue, just as do sensory impulses. *Every idea of a situation tends to produce movements calculated to handle that situation.* This happens just because the discharge of energy from brain center to motor apparatus has become a habit. Constant practice has set up ready paths of discharge between ideational and motor centers. Thus I do not have to deliberately trace out the form of these letters as I write. I simply think the word and, by fixing my attention on the point of the pencil, guide it in straight lines across the page. But the letters form themselves. The simple idea of the word carries itself out into the act of writing it. The interesting and, to the uninitiated, mystifying performances of the planchette, the Ouija board, the automatic writer, the muscle reader, and similar phenomena have been clearly shown to be due to this motor issue of conscious

PRINCIPLES OF APPEAL AND RESPONSE

or subconscious ideas and images in the mind of the experimenter.

Ideas and images of objects, persons and situations tend just as strongly to set up responses calculated to adapt the organism to the particular object, person or situation thought of. Think intently of your cravat, and you will find yourself fingering and adjusting it. Concentrate on the choice cigar in your pocket, and you will likely search at once for the match box. Vividly recall the pleasant languor of a warm bath or the tremendous wind currents of lower Broadway and you will find yourself either stretching out your legs, closing your eyes and reclining in your chair, or, as the case may be, ducking down into your coat collar and clutching your hat brim; and the more you attend to the idea in mind the more completely will its motor issue be realized. If you attend strongly enough you may find the idea amounting to an hallucination—that is, you act just as you would in the presence of the actual object.

This, then, is the fundamental law of ideomotor action, and the basis of what we sometimes call suggestion. *Every idea of a function tends to realize itself, and will do so in so far as it is not inhibited by rival ideas or impeded by physi-*

PROVOKING THE RESPONSE

cal circumstances. Whatever tends to clarify or intensify the image or idea tends to precipitate the act. This is what was meant in the fourth chapter, when it was said that "attention is the basis of every act of will." An idea, once introduced into consciousness, derives its "will power," its action strength, from the degree to which it can completely dominate consciousness. This domination will depend partly on the intrinsic intensity and impulsiveness of the idea, partly on the degree to which it is reinforced by inner processes—attention, ideal, etc. Other things being equal, this power depends on the amount of attention the idea receives.

When such an idea originates more or less directly or spontaneously in the mind of the actor, we call it an *intention,* a *purpose,* an *impulse,* etc. When its origin can be traced further back to some more or less obvious external source, a picture, a command or an invitation of a second person, the behavior of another person or group of persons, etc., we call it a *suggestion.* Suggestion, then, is no more a mystery than the fact that I can speak or write my thoughts, button my coat or sharpen my lead pencil at pleasure. But just as there are certain laws which experiment and general observation show to control the maximum efficiency of voluntary action, so there are certain conditions on which the action power of suggestion depends. We shall enumerate the most important of these conditions and illustrate them by examples in the field of advertising.

THE LAWS OF SUGGESTION

1. *Decision* is only another name for the final outcome of the rivalry of competing ideas. *It is, then, important, in appealing over the short circuit for a specific line of action, not to suggest interference, not to suggest an opposing action, a substitute, a rival idea.* Any such suggestion will simply impede the action power of the first idea, by inviting comparison and making necessary a more or less deliberate choice. This will immediately involve long circuit response, the direct appeal will be reduced to "reason why" copy, and the original purpose of the suggestion will be defeated. It is not necessary to give examples of the violation or observance of this law.

2. The strength of a suggestion will be the greater the more the suggestion appears to be of *spontaneous internal origin.* Every one of us is predisposed in favor of his own ideas. We instinctively resist encroachment, domination, ex-

ternal control. But we welcome and magnify an impulse, a tendency, a line of action that seems to have originated in our own bosom. For this reason an external suggestion which seeks maximal action power should be addressed to some present interest, personal value or universal instinct. Such appeals are not readily recognized as external and foreign. They are readily assimilated and transformed into personal intentions. Two common tendencies of current advertising take advantage of this principle. One is the tendency to give *news interest* to advertising copy. The advertisement thus easily appears as simply an avenue of information, the beseeching or the arrogant tones are lost, and the action suggested seems easily to be a quite natural and matter-of-fact intention of the reader. The other tendency is the constant use of repetition and variation. By these means the particular time and place of origin of the suggestion are lost. So long as I can say, "This or that suggestion comes from this or that advertisement," the appeal remains external and foreign. But when that same appeal has met me in a score of places and in a score of forms, the particular source fades into an indefinite and apparently universal one, a perfectly familiar one, so familiar, indeed, that the

PRINCIPLES OF APPEAL AND RESPONSE

suggestion seems to have been with me all my life, it appears to be an idea of my own, a plan which I have always harbored, and I am surprised that I have delayed its execution so long. The growing practice of signing advertising copy must certainly work against this second law of suggestion, and is hence utterly unsuited for direct appeals, though perhaps no impediment to "reason why" copy. The Hand Sapolio crusade began with the simple command "Be Clean," expressed in various forms and places. The constant presence of this injunction is said to have unconsciously raised the standard of personal cleanliness, and made a market in the locality for Hand Sapolio. Obviously if this crusade had been flagrantly conducted, or associated definitely with a given signboard or placard, the exhortation would have been resented, rather than complied with.

3. The action power of a suggestion depends, among other things, on its actual *intrinsic intensity, force and vigor*. The motor response to an image is not so strong as that to an actual impression. But the more an image comes to resemble an impression, the more intense and insistent it becomes, the stronger becomes the response. Hence the suggestion should be as definite, pointed, incisive and vigorous as it can be

while yet conforming to the second law. It should ring with confidence, certainty and conviction. The action suggested should be specific, clear and full of necessity. Thos. E. Dockrell, in a trenchant essay on this law, has pointed out its confirmation in history, literature and business, at the same time recognizing the distinction between "domination" and "arrogance"—emphasizing thereby the necessity of conforming to the second law as well as to the third. See in this connection also Scott's chapter on "The Direct Command."

4. Suggestion is most active at its *positive* pole. Whenever possible, the human mind works in terms of positives rather than negatives, similarities rather than differences, presences rather than absences. Ask a group of men to compare two buildings in height, two noises in intensity, two towns in size, two men with respect to their efficiency. Nine out of ten will tell you which is the highest, the loudest, the largest or the ablest. Only rarely will you find a man who thinks in terms of shortness, faintness, smallness or weakness. Just as association leads forward more strongly than backward, so attention, judgment and interest are drawn to the positives, the affirmatives, the similarities of the world. We say

PRINCIPLES OF APPEAL AND RESPONSE

things differ in length, strength, importance, not in shortness, weakness, insignificance. Even when an appeal is couched in negative terms, its positive suggestion is more likely to be realized than its negative. The Old Covenant with its "Thou shalt not" had to be replaced by the New Covenant with its simple positive "Thou shalt."

Münsterberg tells a story of an alchemist who sold directions for turning eggs into gold. The buyer was to hold a pan containing the yolks of a dozen eggs, and stir these eggs for half an hour without ever thinking of the word "hippopotamus." Thousands tried, but none succeeded in resisting the positive suggestion. The same writer continues: "Whether shop girls in a department store are advised to ask after every sale 'Do you want to take it with you?' or 'Do you want it sent?' makes no difference to the feeling of the customers, but may mean for the store a difference of thousands for the delivery service."

5. The strength of a suggestion will depend also on the *degree of attention* under which it operates. This law follows naturally from the second and third laws in which the importance of intensity and clearness was pointed out. If you will recall the enumeration of the laws and results of attention you will remember that the

processes attended to becomes both clearer and more intense than it would otherwise be. And since intensity and clearness influence to so marked a degree the action-power of a suggestion, the importance of attention is obvious.

Even when the suggestion is subliminal, that is, below the threshold of consciousness, it possesses action power, and this action power will depend on the variability or constancy of the attention given to the general field in which the stimulus occurs. The writer has often been told by active copy men that the psychological subtleties in advertising are a mere pastime, since the genuine power of advertisements comes from the unconscious influence which they exert on the reader's mind rather than on any conscious mental process set up. It need only be said that in so far as there are such things as unconscious suggestions they operate according to the same laws as do suggestions of which we are keenly aware. These laws of attention, perception, interest, association, memory, choice and action apply to both with equal rigor.

One of the writer's students has recently performed experiments which clearly illustrate the dependence of even unconscious suggestion on degree of attention. It is a well-known fact that

PRINCIPLES OF APPEAL AND RESPONSE

the addition of wing lines pointing in opposite directions may change the apparent length of a base line. Thus the base line in A seems longer

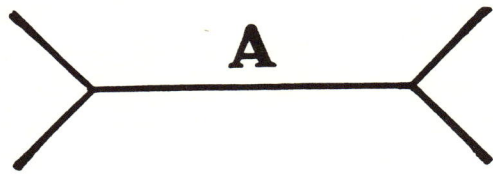

than in B, although they are really of the same length. Practically everybody gets this illusion, which depends upon the strength of some suggestion coming from the added wings. Take the wings away and the lines at once appear equal. What now would be the result if the wings were

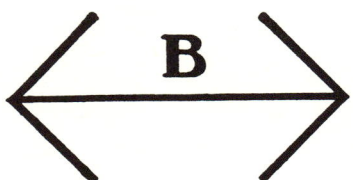

really present, but were drawn so faintly that the observer, at the distance at which he is placed in the experiment, cannot detect them, but sees only the broad strong base line? The suggestion afforded by the wings is present on the retina, but too faint and weak to come to consciousness. The experiment here referred to shows that even under these conditions 17 out of 20 observers yield to the suggestion and pronounce A longer than B. Yet at the end of the experiment of 50 trials for each observer, not one of them even suspected the presence of the wings. They merely thought themselves to be judging the length of two simple black lines. Certain other investigators have reported similar results.

But some people get the illusion with subconscious wings more strongly and frequently than others. The table on page 232 shows the per cent. of the total trials in which each observer pronounced A to be longer than B. In such a table 50 per cent. will mean that no illusion is present, but that, being compelled to choose between A and B, the chances are even. But every per cent. above 50 will indicate the presence of the illusion due to the subconscious suggestion. It will be seen that only three observers have 50 per cent. records or lower, the others ranging upward to as high as 76 per cent., the average being 60 per cent.

How can we explain these striking individual differences? Comparison of these records with the scholarship record for the course of study which these people were taking at the time shows high correlation between the scholarship grade

PRINCIPLES OF APPEAL AND RESPONSE

and the illusion record. People who get the illusion strongly are the people with high grades, people with firm and steady attention habits. The people whose illusion records are low are those whose scholarship is also low. The records of the

TABLE XII

Individual	Per Centage of Times Illusion Occurred
1	76
2	73
3	72
4	68
5	67
6	66
7	66
8	65
9	65
10	63
11	62
12	60
13	58
14	57
15	57
16	52
17	52
18	50
19	50
20	44

experimenter made during the trials also show that those observers who paid close attention to the task were the ones who were most influenced by the suggestion. It follows, then, that even the unconscious influence of appeals will depend on the degree and duration of attention to the general field in which the suggestion appears.

PROVOKING THE RESPONSE

6. The action power of a suggestion will depend furthermore on the *prestige* of its source. The currents and trends of imitation in social life are perfect examples of this law. Custom, style, innovations, always trickle downward from the higher social strata. The butler apes his lordship and the sewing girl her mistress. In logic and politics and many other places the "argumemtum ad hominem" is a dangerous fallacy. This argument proceeds by saying, for instance, that "man is immortal because Sir Oliver Lodge says he is." The more we revere a speaker for one reason or another, the greater confidence we tend to put in what he has to say on any topic whatsoever and the more prone we are to imitate him and to follow out his suggestions. In hypnotic experiments, the subject, it is said, must be *en rapport* with the operator, must have utter confidence and faith in him if the experiment is to work.

Similarly in laboratory tests of the persuasive value of different types of advertising copy, all investigators, Gale, Scott, Strong and the writer, for example, find that such things as the reliability of the firm, the reputation for straight dealing, the length of time which the firm has survived competition, etc., stand out clearly in direct ap-

PRINCIPLES OF APPEAL AND RESPONSE

peals which the experiment declares to be effective.

7. Closely related to the foregoing principle is the law that the strength of a suggestion will be determined partly by the amount of *internal resistance* which the suggestion encounters. Suggestions to violate lifelong habits, firmly fixed moral feelings, sacred relationships, are impotent even during the hypnotic trance. So in advertising, the attempt to displace habits, usages and practices of long standing by simple suggestion, affirmation or assertion, is a heavy one. The suggestion will be most effective when it can call to its aid some other interest or impulse with which it can coöperate.

8. Finally, the strength of a suggestion will depend on the *frequency* with which it is met. Impression after impression may summate themselves to produce a final intensity greater by far than any single stimulus could be. The rôle of repetition in attention, interest, association and memory we have already pointed out. And here, in the field of action, we find it to have equal if not even greater importance. No better illustration of this principle can be found than the parable of "the borrowing friend." The claims of prestige, sympathy and friendship all failed to

PROVOKING THE RESPONSE

secure the three loaves, but persistence, simple repetition did the work. "I say unto you, though he will not rise and give him, *because he is his friend,* yet *because of his importunity* he will rise and give him as many as he needeth" (St. Luke, XI, 8).

But while repetition is effective, it is at the same time expensive, and hence should not be employed indiscriminately. Repetition should be frequent enough to keep the appeal always fresh in the memory. More than this amount is likely to be superfluous. What, then, will be the most economical distribution of repetitions? In a general way it may be said that the distribution of repetitions should conform to the normal curve of forgetting, which has already been described.

But it should be pointed out and clearly borne in mind that mere mechanical repetition avails little unless the repeated stimulus is attended to with more or less interest. For example, give some one a list of fifty words and request him to name, as quickly as possible, the opposites or synonyms of all the words on the list. Repeat this day after day until the observer has read through the list say 25 or 50 times. Then ask him to name or write down the original list of stimulus words which the card contains. You may be surprised to learn that only ten or twelve of the fifty words can be given in three to five minutes, and that even in a quarter of an hour the observer will be unable to recall more than about half of the list. He has repeatedly read through the list, that is, mechanical repetition has been present, but he has not read with the *determination to remember,* that is, his interest has not been in the original list, but in the opposites or synonyms which he was required to give. Now give the observer a new list of words, ask him to read them through with the intention of remembering them, and you will find that after a very few repetitions he can repeat the whole list correctly. Mere mechanical repetition, that is to say, is as futile as mere mechanical intensity, magnitude or contrast. Only when repetition is accompanied by *interest* is it likely to be worth what it costs.

CHAPTER XIII

INSTINCTS, THEIR NATURE AND STRENGTH

In the history of the race certain objects or situations in the world have stood out as fundamentally important factors in the struggle for survival, for supremacy and for comfort. Further, definite kinds of response have been proven to be most appropriate in dealing with these objects. Individuals who have reacted promptly and definitely in these appropriate ways have been successful, have flourished, and have left descendants who possessed the same inborn tendencies to reaction. Individuals who for one reason or another failed to react in these appropriate ways perished. The result has been a constant selection of those individuals who possess more and more firmly the natural mechanical tendency to react in the way which race history has proven to be appropriate. These reactions in their finally developed form are called *instincts*.

We may look upon the *instinct* as a very complicated *reflex action*. Just as the eyelid reflexly

PRINCIPLES OF APPEAL AND RESPONSE

blinks when a blow is struck, without the volition of the owner, so the organism behaves reflexly in definitely useful ways in the presence of certain kinds of objects. The sight of one boy sets up the pugilistic attitude on the part of another. The presence of her child leads the normal mother to varied acts of caressing, nursing and protecting. The discovery of a rich gold deposit attracts men from all parts of the world, who dig out ore and hide it away in secret places, just as a bird hides pieces of twine, a water rat all manner of stray objects. The discovery of a remedy for a hitherto incurable disease sets all the world a-talking and a-buying.

These actions we say come so promptly and universally because of the common *instincts* which men possess, instincts of pugnacity, rivalry, maternal love, accumulation, acquisition, self-dependence, curiosity, play, construction, economy, sympathy, imitation, family affection, social cooperation, display, sexual mating, hunting, hospitality, civic and national pride, leadership, etc., etc.

From the point of view of the advertiser, the important thing is that if an appeal can but touch off one of these instinct mechanisms it is sure of at once possessing attention power, interest, imagery, association and memory value, and is extremely likely to set up strong response. And the stronger and more universal the instinct, the greater the likelihood of its effectiveness. Most articles can be described so as to appeal to any one of a wide range of instincts. Thus an ordinary article, such as a clothes-dryer, can be emphasized as cheap, as safe, as popular, as home-made, as amusing, as clean, etc. An advertisement of the Hill Clothes Dryer, wretchedly constructed from the artistic point of view, nevertheless presented an argument which appealed strongly to the universal interest in bodily safety. In an experiment on the relative persuasiveness of 75 subway cards the writer found this card to be unanimously the most convincing of the series. And he is informed that the copy has produced gratifying results from the point of view of sales.

Twenty years ago advertisements failed to recognize the specific character of instincts; appeals tended to be of a vague, generalized sort which in our day would pass unobserved by a busy public. But the present practice is more and more to recognize the specific instinct as a basis of appeal, and to concentrate the appeal strongly on a single instinct rather than to distribute it among many. The following pairs of advertisements reprinted

PRINCIPLES OF APPEAL AND RESPONSE

from *Advertising and Selling* clearly show this tendency. Compare the vague, generalized copy of 1890 with the definite pointed appeals of twenty years later.

We shall take up, in a moment, the question of the relative strength of these specific instincts as

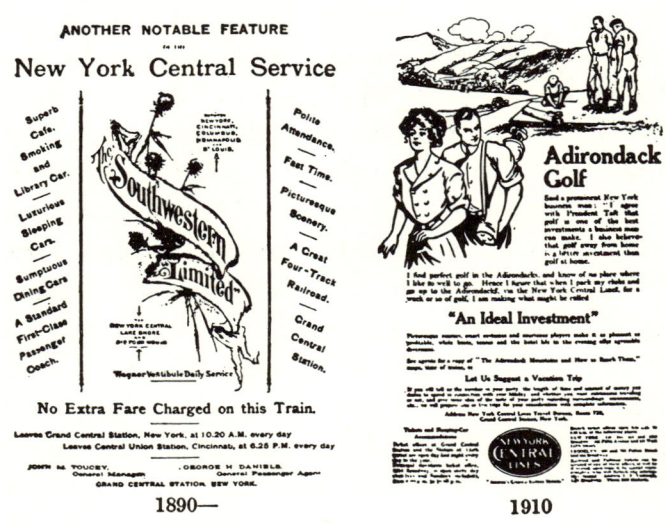

1890— 1910

a basis of appeal in advertising. But before passing to this problem, it is necessary to point out another important group of factors, which, while they can scarcely be called instincts, yet closely resemble them in character. The instinct we are born with. It is the result of the experience of our ancestors. But during our own lives

INSTINCTS, THEIR NATURE AND STRENGTH

we all come to acquire certain other prompt reactions to the particular things in our experience.

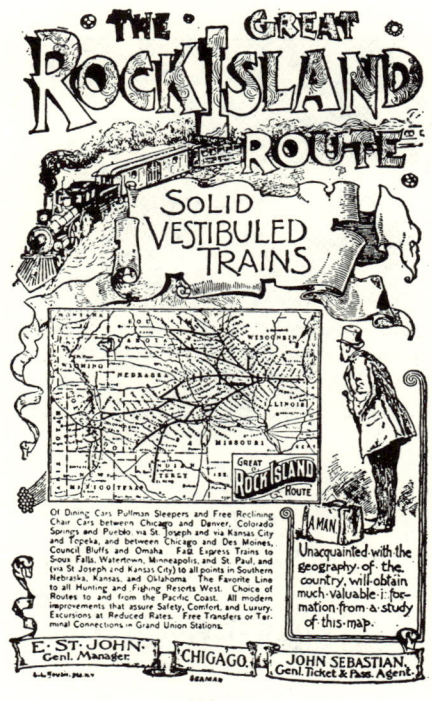

1890—

Thus, the moment a thing can be demonstrated to be *chic,* stylish, nobby, modern, popular, clean, artistic, imported, scientifically made, guaranteed, elegant, socially advantageous, progressive, gentlemanly, bohemian, refined, sporty, up-to-

PRINCIPLES OF APPEAL AND RESPONSE

date, used by some favorite, etc., etc., it will at once find a market of greater or less extent and permanence.

1910

Let us call these ideas *effective conceptions*. The general law is: Besides our instinctive actions our conduct roots largely in a few fundamental conceptions, ideas, values, standards, which we apply as action criteria. The moment

INSTINCTS, THEIR NATURE AND STRENGTH

an appeal, a suggestion, an object, can be classified under one or other of these headings, our attitude toward it is determined. Throw an atmosphere of elegance, of style or of healthfulness

1890—

1910

about clothing, breakfast foods, soaps, musical instruments, etc., as the case may be, and the reader will at once react to it by "short circuit" response, either favorably or unfavorably, according as the conception used is in his particular case *effective* or *weak*. Since these *effective conceptions* are in their action similar to *instincts,* we may group the two together in our attempt to learn how these differ among themselves in strength and action-power, how these differences vary with sex, age, class, occupation, commodity, etc. We must say to begin with that this is at present a field which is almost unworked experimentally. General comments and opinions are abundant, and they are just about as reliable as such random observations usually are. The experimental results which we shall report will, then, represent pioneer investigations of their kind, and must be held subject to such modification and correction as later investigation shall suggest.

So far we have emphasized only the principles controlling the direct appeal to "short circuit" response. There remains yet the "reason why" appeal to comparison, argument and deliberate choice, to the "long circuit" action of reason. It is evidently impossible to say in general terms what sorts of arguments, what methods of reasoning, what sort of "selling points" or "reasons" will be effective. These facts will vary with the type of article advertised, with the type of man appealed to, and with the actual points of superiority which the goods may chance to possess. But it may be said that even in our reasoning it is the appeal to *our own* point of view, *our own* dominant instincts, conceptions, values,

INSTINCTS, THEIR NATURE AND STRENGTH

habits and needs that constitutes the most effective argument. The answer to the question of the relative value of types of argument, selling points, etc., may then be left to the experiments which are to follow.

Since the short circuit appeal is based on the fact that human beings are equipped with certain instinctive tendencies to react in definite ways toward particular objects or situations, it follows that this type of appeal is particularly adapted to the case of certain commodities—to those types of articles toward which or toward the use or services of which we react with promptness, certainty, and feeling. And since acquired habits come to resemble instincts in these respects, we may include both habits and instincts as the basis of the short circuit appeal. In a general way we may say that the following principles are true.

The short circuit appeal (display advertisement, appeal to instinct, feeling and habit) is well adapted:

1. For all *personal* articles, the use of which is *intimate* and *private,* as toilet articles, gifts, stationery, etc.

2. For articles of *luxury, display,* and *adorn-*

ment, as jewelry, fancy dress goods, feathers and plumes, flowers, etc.

3. For articles enjoyed *in themselves* or *for their own sake,* rather than for remote service which they may render, as drinks, musical instruments, sweetmeats, toys, etc.

4. For articles calculated to promote the *bodily safety* of the individual or of those dependent on him, as disinfectants, safety devices, insurance, weapons of defence, etc.

5. For *all food products.*

6. For all clothing which tends to be ornamental rather than utilitarian in character, as ties, collars, laces, canes, etc.

The long circuit appeal (reason why copy, argument, comparative statement of advantages, etc.) may also be used to reinforce the strength of many of the short circuit appeals used in such cases as those just enumerated. But it is especially fitted, by its nature and by the way in which it will be reacted to, for articles which are the reverse of these in character; for articles which are in themselves, or from the use to which they are put, impersonal, utilitarian, instrumental; and for articles which are intended not so much to fill present needs only, but also to create new needs or desires—such articles as books, plows, buttons,

INSTINCTS, THEIR NATURE AND STRENGTH

hammers, trucks, etc.—in general, to those things which partake of the nature of a *tool*.

It is further true that not all instincts are equally strong, not all habits equally coercive. This being the case, information concerning the relative strength of various possible appeals to interest, attention, instinct and response tendencies is desirable. To men who desire to make their copy or their selling talk effective, and at the same time economical, the question of the relative strength of appeals, instincts, interests and effective habits is a live one. The writer has repeatedly been asked by such men to state the relative strength of various appeals in the case of the average man—to say in how far certain interests are universal, to what degree certain general types are pronounced, and how they are distributed and conditioned by age, sex, race, etc. The practical man expects the expert psychologist to possess such information, and he has the right to expect much more than we are at present able to tell him.

Only one or two fragmentary attempts have been made to answer such questions experimentally. Thus Harlow Gale studied a series of soap advertisements by the method of questionnaire and voluntary introspection. His results,

PRINCIPLES OF APPEAL AND RESPONSE

when worked over into terms of relative position, would yield some such result as the following. The smaller the number the higher the position, hence the stronger the appeal.

TABLE XIII

Appeal	Relative Position	
	Men	Women
Purity by government's test..........	2.46	2.29
Old firm.............................	2.68	2.11
Home industry......................	3.22	3.49
"Attractiveness"....................	3.50	3.49
Special sale........................	3.68	4.06
Souvenir prize......................	4.62	3.47

The manager of a western magazine, as reported by Scott, secured thousands of replies from readers as to which advertisement for a given month had interested them most, and why. The following table resulted:

TABLE XIV

Reason	Number of replies
Reliability of firm or goods.....................	607
Money considerations, cheapness................	508
Beauty of the advertisement....................	418
Presented goods needed at the time.............	408

Obviously such meager and generalized results are of little value. What is needed is a series of

INSTINCTS, THEIR NATURE AND STRENGTH

TABLE XV

Breakfast Foods

APPEAL	Avge.	P. E.
Purity	5.6	.4
Doctor's Recommendation	7.5	.5
Taste No. 1	8.6	.5
Food Quality	9.1	.6
Taste No. 2	9.2	.5
Healthful	9.3	.4
Brain Power	9.4	.5
Old Firm	9.8	.5
Magnifying Glass (Health)	9.9	.4
Mental Dullness	10.2	.5
Roosevelt Recommendation	10.3	.6
Shot from Gun	10.3	.5
Used Everywhere	10.4	.4
Men Like It	11.0	.4
Necessary as Turkey on Thanksgiving	11.4	.5
Home Industry	12.2	.5
Royalty	12.4	.5
Enormous Plant	12.8	.6
Souvenir Free	14.5	.4
	15.8	.4

Average Position in a Series of Twenty Appeals, both with and without pictures Group of Fifty Men and Women of Varying Class, Education, Color and Age

Avge.=Average position of the Fifty Judgments

P. E. = Probable Error or Reliability of Average

Table shows the result of an experiment, in which the appeals were specifically stated to be advertisements of BREAKFAST FOODS. These appeals were also arranged by fifty persons, and the table gives the average for the fifty. No pictures were used in these appeals, the words alone serving to direct the appeal to the special interest or instinct concerned. The second column gives the Probable Error of the average. Thus, taking Doctor's Recommendation as a sample, its average is 7.5, and its probable error .5. This means that the value is not absolutely 7.5, but may go up as high as 7.5+.5 or 7.0, or that it may go down as low as 7.5+.5, or to 8.0. The numbers in each case indicate the average value in a series of twenty appeals, the smaller the number the stronger the appeal.

249

rigorous test experiments, under conditions which are constant, and by methods which will afford comparative numerical measures.

Strong has reported experiments designed to determine the relative value of various arguments in favor of a given type of commodity by securing typical advertisements of such articles and using the methods which were referred to in the first chapter of this book and which are to be described in detail in the chapter which is to follow. His studies include such special articles as vacuum cleaners, pianos, breakfast foods, and soaps. An interesting presentation and interpretation of his results is given in his doctor's dissertation on "The Relative Merits of Advertisements." The preceding tabulation of the results of the series of breakfast food appeals will serve as an example of the suggestive information which such experiments yield.

Studies of the sort reported by Gale, Scott and Strong (some of Strong's experiments have been subsequently repeated and confirmed by Starch, with clothing advertisements) are especially useful as pointing the way toward the possibility of a complete exploration of the range of human interests and instincts. In the following chapter will be given an account of such an attempt, which in point of time antedated the experiments of Strong and Starch, but which logically follows upon them. We shall there present a series of measurements which apply, not to special articles, but to all articles in general, arranged in such a way that the relative value of various appeals for any specified commodity may be approximately determined by reference to the larger table.

It should be said here that we are not interested, in this connection, with the strength of the various instincts and interests in phases of life other than that of the business transaction. Nor can knowledge of the strength of the various instinctive tendencies as they display themselves in the home, the school, or in sport, serve as a basis for determination of the strength of the same instinctive tendencies when they constitute reactions to business appeals. Thus one might be exceedingly vain and much concerned with his personal appearance in a general way, and yet mistrust appeals in the way of advertisements and selling talks based upon such an instinct. One might be sedulously careful of his health, so far as his own activity might be concerned, and yet mistrust assertions of the health-promoting qualities of any advertised article of commerce. And an individual with strong imitative tendencies with respect to his general behavior might yet refuse to adopt a given article or style of dress merely because some favorite opera singer or public official had recommended it.

CHAPTER XIV

THE RELATIVE STRENGTH OF THE CHIEF INSTINCTS AND INTERESTS

Before taking up the main topic of this chapter, it will be well to consider in some detail the method by which the results here presented were secured. We have frequently had occasion to refer to methods of measuring the strength of such subjective things as the strength of appeals, the persuasiveness of advertisements, etc. How, now, is it possible to measure these subjective factors, so long as there is no objective scale with which they may be compared? A few illustrations may throw light on the problem.

Suppose that I have in my laboratory a series of weights which differ from each other by very small amounts. Suppose, further, that I desire to know the relative weight of the members of the series, but have no balance with which to weigh them, and that the differences between those most like each other are so small that I cannot absolutely trust to my judgments when I lift

PRINCIPLES OF APPEAL AND RESPONSE

the weights in my hand and compare them with each other. I may be led to mistrust my judgments because I do not always judge consistently, or because the judgments of other people in the laboratory disagree somewhat with mine. These conditions being given, is it possible for me in any way to determine with certainty the order of the weights as that order would turn out if a balance were available? The answer is that it is not only possible, but at the same time very easily accomplished. All I need to do is to let a large number of people, say twenty different individuals, arrange the weights in what seem to them to be the order of their relative heaviness, when lifted in the hand. Then taking the average of the twenty judgments of each weight in the series, I derive a final order based on the combined judgments of the twenty observers. This final order will be found to coincide with the order of heaviness as determined by the balances, when such are available. Anyone who doubts may easily satisfy himself by trying the experiment. If there are, say, seven weights in the series, and five different individuals pass judgments upon them, some such table as the one on page 255 will result:

The order of heaviness, as determined by the judgments of the group of observers, is seen to

STRENGTH OF INSTINCTS AND INTERESTS

afford a correct statement of the real relative heaviness of the series of weights. The objective scale (the balance) is unnecessary. We have used it here only in order to check up the order as de-

TABLE XVI

Typical Table Resulting from Order of Merit Method

The Weights	Position in order of weight, as judged by five persons					Average Position	Order of Heaviness
65 grams	7	6	7	7	7	6.8	1
63 grams	6	7	6	6	5	6.0	2
61 grams	4	5	4	5	6	4.8	3
59 grams	5	4	5	3	4	4.2	4
57 grams	3	2	3	4	3	3.0	5
55 grams	1	3	2	2	1	1.8	6
53 grams	2	1	1	1	2	1.4	7

termined by the judgments. In the same way it is possible to determine the order of intensity of a series of sounds, the relative legibility of specimens of handwriting, the relative length of lines differing only slightly from each other, the relative excellence of literary compositions, the relative eminence of scientific men, the relative persuasiveness of selling talks, the pulling power of advertisements, the strength of various appeals to instincts and interests.

It must be noted that in the experiment on the series of weights, I do not ask my observers to arrange the weights in the order in which they think

PRINCIPLES OF APPEAL AND RESPONSE

they would appear to some other individual, nor in the order in which they think they would appear to people in general, nor even in the order in which they think the weights would be shown to stand when measured on the balance. I instruct each individual, "Arrange the weights in the order of heaviness as they seem to you when you consider them. Arrange them in the order in which they affect you when you lift them." Similarly, if I am studying a series of advertisements, I do not say: "Arrange these appeals in order according to the way in which you think they would affect *other people*," but I say: "Here are a series of appeals. Arrange them in order according to *the degree to which they make you desire the article,* or interest you in it, or incline you favorably toward it." That is to say, I do not ask him to judge whether or not the various appeals are *good advertisements* (persuasive to people in general). Similarly, if I am studying a series of landscapes, I do not ask my observers to arrange them in the order of beauty as they think other people would be affected by them. I merely say: "Which picture is most beautiful *to you?* Put it at the top. Which of the remaining ones is most beautiful? Put it next in order, etc." But my *final* orders of merit *will* represent the way in which people as a whole, in general, on the average, or in the long run, will react to the objects studied. Or if any objective measurement is possible, the final order will coincide with these objective measurements. In other words, the determinations afforded by the experimental methods are *true measures* of the qualities or traits investigated.

This is the method which was used in measuring the relative pulling power of the different series of advertisements discussed in the first chapter of this book. And it was there shown that the results of the laboratory tests actually enabled us to know in advance the relative order of pulling power of the advertisements when they were used in business. It should be said further, that, by the use of the proper precision and statistical method, it is not only possible to determine the relative order of these subjective factors, but to measure the *amount of difference* between the various members of the series. A discussion of these further refinements of the method would involve more technicality than it is the purpose of this book to contain. Readers who may be interested in knowing more about the method, its history, applications, and possibilities, may be referred to Strong's monograph entitled "The Relative Merits of Advertisements." This monograph consists of the elaboration and justification of the method here described, with applications. Thorndike's "Mental and Social Measurements" gives a useful account of the statistical and mathematical points involved in such measurements.

Having given this brief description and justification of the laboratory method, we are now ready for the results of an extensive experiment on the strength of such appeals as may be used in various business situations. In order to get at the strength of the appeal in itself, and independently of any particular article or brand in connection with which it might appear, abstract appeals have been used, which referred not to any commodity in particular, but to an ideal, imaginary article, designated by an abstract symbol, such as 3K7. The value of abstracting from particular commodities will be pointed out after the results have been given. Fifty abstract appeals, each designed to reach a definite and different interest, instinct, or line of argument, were prepared. These appeals were typewritten on separate slips of paper, and presented without being accompanied by picture or illustration. In addition to the statement of the appeal, each card bore a sin-

STRENGTH OF INSTINCTS AND INTERESTS

gle word or pair of words, designed to emphasize the specific character and direction of the appeal, to reinforce the suggestion or argument offered by the text itself, and to insure, in so far as possible, the same attitude on the part of all the observers in the presence of the respective appeals. By employing such material the following results were secured:

1. Each appeal tends to be single and uncomplicated by other interests.
2. Each is divorced from reactions to any article or brand as such.
3. The elimination of illustrations and the use of the same general style and expression lends homogeneity to the group of appeals.
4. A wide range of specialized isolated appeals is secured, which fairly represents the possible range of appeal afforded by human nature.

The series of 50 appeals was given to each observer, along with the following printed directions.

DIRECTIONS

(Read these directions two times, carefully, before beginning the experiment.)

PRINCIPLES OF APPEAL AND RESPONSE

This is an experiment in the psychology of advertising. Its purpose will be explained after you have finished the series. Each card contains an advertisement of some fictitious article, indicated by a letter-numeral symbol (thus, 3K7). It need make no difference what the article might really be. It may be well to assume that all the cards advertise different brands or makes of the same article,—some ideal, imaginary article, to which any or all of the advertisements might apply.

I. Read all the advertisements through and arrange them in five consecutive piles, in an order of merit,— according to their *persuasiveness, i. e.,* according to the degree in which they make you *desire* the article or *convince* you of its merit.

There will thus be five degrees of *persuasiveness,* which might be roughly designated:

1. Most persuasive.
2. Very persuasive.
3. Fairly persuasive.
4. Mildly persuasive.
5. Least persuasive.

Arrange the five piles in a row so that Group 1 is at the top, Group 5 at the bottom, and the three other

STRENGTH OF INSTINCTS AND INTERESTS

groups in their respective positions between these extremes.

II. Having done this turn to the top pile (Group 1) and arrange the advertisements in that group in a strict order of merit,—the strongest in the pile thus getting the first position, the next strongest the second position, and so on.

After the top pile is arranged, treat each of the other groups in the same manner. In this way the whole series of advertisements will have been arranged in an order of merit series with respect to their *persuasiveness,*—with the *most persuasive* at the top and the *least persuasive* at the bottom.

III. Without disturbing your arrangement of the Groups, notify the experimenter that you have completed the series.

The 50 different appeals follow, arranged in a final order of merit for a group of 40 observers, consisting of 20 men and 20 women. The first pair of figures gives the *average value* and *mean variation* for the women, the second pair the measures for the men.

1. 1K6,—SCIENTIFIC:—Our 1K6 article is manufactured by approved scientific methods and by scientifically tested processes, by technically

trained men, working under the constant supervision of experts.

2—9.1; 2—8.4

2. 1W5,—DURABILITY:—Combine utility with durability by using 1W5. It lasts one-third longer than the ordinary article. Stands the wear and tear of constant use, combining equal quality with greater permanence and longer service.

1—8.2; 6—8.0

3. 1F3,—SANITARY:—This is the only sanitary 1F3 on the market. Put up in germ-proof, dust-proof, hermetically sealed packages, and made of strictly pure and unadulterated ingredients.

5—7.7; 3—10.5

4. 2D8,—EFFICIENCY:—Actual energy, earning power, is what counts in modern business. The day is past when recognition rested on pull and social influence. 2D8 will increase your efficiency 25%. By no other means can you secure such prompt and sure increase of producing capacity.

7—12.8; 8—13.7

STRENGTH OF INSTINCTS AND INTERESTS

5. 1T8,—TIME:—Save the minutes and the hours will save themselves. Time is money. Our latest 1T8 is the biggest time saver on the market. Does in twenty minutes what requires, with other brands, a half an hour.

3—8.6; 14—12.2

6. 1N6,—APPETIZING:—Try 1N6. It comes fresh from the field and its appetizing flavor is a treat to the palate. It makes a dainty breakfast, a delightful luncheon, and a delicious dessert.

13—8.9; 5—8.8

7. 2B7,—FAMILY AFFECTION:—A final day must come to every man, and no one wants to see his children left dependent on mere accident. You owe a duty of provision and foresight to your family. A 2B7 will guarantee this comfort and security when you are gone.

17—13.5; 1—7.7

8. 1Z5,—VALUE:—Absolutely superior quality and finer finish. 1Z5 may cost a little more, but it's worth the difference. One trial will convince.

4—7.3; 16—10.1

PRINCIPLES OF APPEAL AND RESPONSE

9. 2L7,—EVOLUTION:—Our latest 2L7 is the result of generations of experience and experiment. After years of trial 2L7 stands distinctly in a class by itself as the final product of a long evolution,—the climax of mechanical genius.

11—10.9; 12—9.1

10. 2C8,—AMBITION:—There's always room higher up. Capable leaders are always in demand. Why stay among the incompetent when 2C8 will bring you a better position and increase your salary. The man who uses 2C8 is sure of recognition and rapid promotion.

6—10.9; 18—13.5

11. 2F6,—SELF-DEFENSE:—Forearmed is forewarned. Your life is always threatened by some lurking danger or another. With 2F6 in your home you are always secure and able to protect the rights and person of yourself and of those whose safety is your chief concern.

15—9.7; 10—11.3

12. 1R4,—REPUTATION:—Established in 1870, we have been for 40 years the leading manufacturers of 1R4 in the country.

STRENGTH OF INSTINCTS AND INTERESTS

We have the longest and most enviable record of any house, in our line, on the continent.

$$9—12.8;\ 21—12.0$$

13. 2E9, — GUARANTEED:—Our well-known trade-mark guarantees quality and satisfaction. All our 2E9 is strictly warranted high grade. Your money refunded if 2E9 does not accomplish all we claim for it.

$$10—12.7;\ 20—11.4$$

14. 1P5,—STIMULATING:—1P5 fortifies the body against the inroads of toil and disease, gives new life and vigor to tired muscles and nerves, and removes unnecessary strain and fatigue.

$$12—9.6;\ 41—19.4$$

15. 1V3,—SAFETY:—Avoid danger by using the only absolutely safety-built, accident-proof 1V3. Do not court danger by taking chances. This is the only 1V3 in which you get all the protection and none of the risk.

$$26—11.5;\ 7—10.2$$

16. 1E5,—POPULAR:—The name is on all tongues. You will find 1E5 in the ladies' dress-

ing-room, in the scholar's study, in the nursery, in kitchens of the humble, in crowded Eastern cities and on limitless Western plains. Used in millions of homes and everywhere it is on top.

29—13.2; 4—9.9

17. 2R5,—ECONOMIZE:—A dollar saved is a dollar earned. 2R5 will save you money. Why not cut down expense items and start a bank account. 2R5 will help you do it.

14—8.0; 19—7.3

18. 1Q3,—MATERNAL LOVE:—Nothing is too good for baby. 1Q3 comforts and soothes the little chap and makes of babyhood one happy play time. Assures the children's health and enjoyment.

18—11.4; 15—11.8

19. 1J4,—MODERNITY:—Strictly up-to-date design with all the latest improvements. 1J4 is equipped with every advantage and ingenious device known to recent invention.

22—8.8; 13—11.6

20. 1C3,—HEALTH:—As a general tonic, 1C3 is unequaled. It nourishes the system, enriches the

STRENGTH OF INSTINCTS AND INTERESTS

blood, builds up firm, healthy tissue and gives tone and color to the whole body. Prevents grippe and pneumonia.

8—10.9; 30—15.6

21. 1X9,—QUALITY:—Why keep on wasting money when for the price of the ordinary article you can get our own superior 1X9. Goes farther and does the work better than any other.

16—12.5; 22—9.5

22. 1A7,—ELEGANCE:—Nothing contributes so strongly to the luxurious comfort of the modern home as 1A7. Its presence gives dignity and elegance to the whole and creates an atmosphere of daintiness and distinction.

30—10.9; 11—10.3

23. 1G2,—BARGAIN:—No 1G2 was ever offered before for the money. As good as any others and only two-thirds their cost. We are enabled to offer this proposition only by virtue of our mammoth plant and enormous capacity. Why pay more?

28—11.0; 17—12.0

PRINCIPLES OF APPEAL AND RESPONSE

24. 2Q7,—SYMPATHY:—Kindness is the first law of humanity. Much of the pain and discomfort inflicted on dumb animals could be relieved by using 2Q7. Be humane to your beast. Use 2Q7.

$$37—15.3;\ 9—9.9$$

25. 2O8,—NECESSARY:—You cannot afford to do without 2O8. It is indispensable in your home, in your business, in your recreation. Every man, woman and child needs it constantly.

$$20—8.2;\ 27—14.0$$

26. 2W8,—MIDDLEMEN:—Why pay middlemen's profit? Buy direct from the manufacturer and keep the profits yourself. We make 2W8 and ship straight to the consumer.

$$23—11.7;\ 26—10.4$$

27. 2Z7,—COURTESY:—Nothing is more discourteous than an offensive breath.

2Z7 cleanses the system, purifies the blood and sweetens the breath.

$$27—10.1;\ 25—12.0$$

28. 2T9,—REMARKABLE GROWTH:—The superior quality of 2T9 is demonstrated by the rapid development of our business.

STRENGTH OF INSTINCTS AND INTERESTS

    Total Capital, 1890,— $15,273.00
      "   "   1895,—   85,896.00
      "   "   1900,—   240,142.00
      "   "   1905,—   703,279.00
      "   "   1910,— 3,875,639.00

              19—16.3; 36—11.5

29.   1S6,—AMUSEMENT:—Don't look bored! Buy 1S6. The most side-splitting, mirth-provoking novelty ever devised. Amuses old and young. Affords fun and laughter from morning till night.

              34—10.7; 23—10.6

30.   2X4,—HOSPITALITY:—Don't be content with envying the successful hostess when you can secure the same keen pleasure for yourself. The homes equipped with 2X4 are known far and wide for their generous comfort and open hospitality.

              24—8.0; 34—11.0

31.   2Y9,—YOUTH:—The fountain of eternal youth has never been discovered, but it has been demonstrated beyond a doubt that 2Y9 restores youthful vigor, quickens the step and gives new life to both body and mind.

              24—8.9; 34—13.1

PRINCIPLES OF APPEAL AND RESPONSE

32. 2V7—HUNTING:—Just the thing for the fishing and hunting trip. Ensures a lively spirit in the field and solid comfort in the camp. No vacation outfit is complete without 2V7.

31—12.1; 28—11.6

33. 1O9,—SOCIAL STANDING:—The use of 1O9 is the stamp of the gentleman. It is always found where social standards are high, and is the favorite of men and women of discriminating taste and culture.

38—9.0; 24—12.6

34. 2S8,—ENORMOUS:—We have the largest establishment engaged in the production of 2S8 in the United States.

Capital, $12,000,000.00.

Factories or branch establishments in every prominent city in the country.

25—14.6; 38—11.4

35. 1Y2,—CHEAP:—Buy 1Y2. Costs just one-half the price of its competitors. Why spend two days' wages when one day's work will bring our high-class article to your home?

32—10.1; 33—9.6

STRENGTH OF INSTINCTS AND INTERESTS

36. 2J9,—GET THE GENUINE:—Avoid substitutes. Many may pattern after us, but none can equal us. As a matter of fact 2J9 has many imitators, but there is only one standard, genuine article. Ask for 2J9.

21—12.0; 48—9.4

37. 2P6,—PROGRESS:—Don't be a dead one. Use 2P6 and be up to date. It is an essential part of every progressive modern establishment.

40—11.7; 29—12.3

38. 2A3,—SALE:—We are closing out our large stock of 2A3 at a great sacrifice, to make way for next year's goods. For the next ten days 2A3 will be sold at less than cost. Come early. Don't miss this rare opportunity.

41—11.3; 31—11.7

39. 2M5,—EXCEL:—Don't be a wall flower. Use 2M5 and you will be the envy of all your friends. It gives that look of superiority which everyone recognizes and respects, but which few possess.

36—11.7; 42—13.0

40. 2K4,—CIVIC PRIDE:—We appeal to your civic pride. 2K4 is made in your own city, by

PRINCIPLES OF APPEAL AND RESPONSE

local workmen and backed by strictly home capital. Encourage home industry. Use 2K4.

33—15.0; 45—10.3

41. 1H9,—PATRIOTISM:—Our 1H9 product is made for American consumers, of strictly American-grown materials, by an American firm employing exclusively American labor and American capital.

35—15.6; 43—10.3

42. 2G4,—UNION MADE:—We stand for organized labor. 2G4 is a strictly union-made product, built by union labor, of union-raised material, and sold exclusively by all union dealers.

49—14.6; 32—11.6

43. 1M8,—RECOMMENDATION:—Here's what the world-famous tenor of the Metropolitan Opera House says of 1M8:

"I have used your product constantly and have continued to derive great benefit from it."

(Signed) ENRICO CARUSO.

46—14.0; 37—14.5

44. 1D8,—NOBBY:—Our 1D8 products are made by our smartest designers, especially for those

272

who love nobby and dressy styles. Exclusive patterns and dashing cuts, unequaled in snap and color.

48—7.3; 35—10.3

45. 1B5,—STYLE:—Our new 1B5 is fresh from the center of fashion, representing the latest creation of accepted artists of style, in exclusive designs and dressy patterns, *chic* and strictly *à la mode.*

47—5.8; 40—7.5

46. 1L7,—ROYALTY:—1L7 will be found in most of the houses of European royalty. We are commissioned by official warrant to supply 1L7 to his Excellency, the Emperor of Germany.

50—8.5; 39—12.1

47. 2N7,—ADMIRATION:—Do you desire the admiration of those you meet? Use 2N7 and you will be the constant center of attraction to adoring and envious eyes. No jewels or marvels of costuming can add so much to your appearance as 2N7.

43—9.4'; 47—11.5

48. 2H8,—IMPORTED:—All 2H8 products are strictly imported and foreign stamped. 2H8 comes straight from European makers, and its superior quality is thereby guaranteed.

45—10.0; 46—9.8

49. 1U4,—BEAUTY:—Are you as pretty as you might be? No one wants to be homely. The continued use of 1U4 removes the undesirable blemish, beautifies the complexion, renders the form attractive and gives charm to the figure.

42—8.9; 50—9.8

50. 2U3,—PERSONALITY:—Everyone desires to be attractive to the opposite sex. 2U3 will give you distinctive presence and engaging personality which is irresistible in its appeal.

44—10.9; 49—19.2

Certain sources of "error" in such an experiment are at once obvious:

1. It is difficult to keep out of even the abstract appeals some suggestion of special reference. Thus the appeal to *appetite* will inevitably suggest food, some *health* appeals are strikingly medicinal in tone, and doubtless in most cases there is a more or less pronounced tendency to think of one article rather than another.

STRENGTH OF INSTINCTS AND INTERESTS

2. There is a certain feeling of self-consciousness and reserve in submitting honestly to such an experiment, a tendency to place low certain appeals which really bulk large outside of the laboratory, or a tendency toward ideal arrangement strongly suggestive of the inclination to give learned responses in association tests.

Of these two sources of error, it may be said that from the practical point of view only the second is of importance. And that the danger here is minimal is attested by the fact that the results of such tests are verified by keyed results. The observers used were 30 women, mostly Juniors in Barnard College, taking their second year's work in psychology, and 20 men in Columbia College of corresponding age and class. Twenty of the women made two arrangements, one month apart, without meanwhile having seen the cards. The other 10 women and the 20 men made but one arrangement. No time limit was given. Each observer was allowed to work over the material until a satisfactory order had been secured.

Comparison of the two trials of the group of 20 women will thus throw light on the permanence of such judgments and on the constancy of different individuals. Comparison of this group with the group of 10 women will show how far the average judgments of such an experiment are typical of the results to be expected from observers of approximately the same class. Comparison of the group of men with the group of the women will reveal such sex differences in these traits as may be present. Separate study of each group will show the degree of variability introduced by the personal equations of the various observers, the general relationships of individual judgments to group averages, etc. The array of figures yielded by such an experiment is a veritable mine of suggestions and material. These results from the point of view of the applied psychologist merit discussion in detail. For the present, however, we must limit ourselves to giving the various tables of measures and briefly summarizing their meaning and significance for advertising and selling.

The table gives a statement of the relative persuasiveness of the different appeals for men and women, their average values and positions. In this table the various cards which might be classed under one general heading, such as *health, reputation, economy,* etc., have been grouped and their average taken as representing the most probable value of that general type of appeal. The second column in the table gives, for each general type, the number of actual cards

TABLE XVII

Relative Persuasiveness for Men and Women

Appeal	No.	40 Final		20 Women		20 Men	
		Av.	Pos.	Av.	Pos.	Av.	Pos.
Health............	3	4.0	1	5.0	2	3.0	1
Cleanliness........	1	4.0	2	5.0	3	3.0	2
Scientific..........	2	6.5	3	6.5	5	7.0	5
Time Saved........	1	8.5	4	3.0	1	14.0	10
Appetizing.........	1	9.0	5	13.0	8	5.0	3
Efficiency.........	3	9.5	6	5.3	4	13.3	9
Safety............	4	10.5	7	15.7	11	5.2	4
Durability.........	2	11.5	8	8.5	6	14.0	11
Quality...........	2	14.5	9½	10.0	7	19.0	13
Modernity.........	2	14.5	9½	16.5	12	12.5	8
Family Affection...	4	15.2	11	21.8	15	8.7	6
Reputation........	5	21.1	12	18.4	13	32.8	15
Guarantee.........	2	21.2	13	14.5	9	28.0	19
Sympathy.........	1	23.0	14	37.0	23	9.0	7
Medicinal.........	3	25.0	15	15.0	10	35.0	22
Imitation..........	3	25.5	16	30.0	19	21.0	14
Elegance..........	2	26.0	17	34.0	22	17.5	12
Courtesy..........	1	26.0	18	27.0	17	25.0	16
Economy..........	5	26.4	19	27.6	18	35.2	17
Affirmation........	2	29.0	20	30.0	20	28.0	20
Sport.............	2	29.0	21	32.5	21	25.5	18
Hospitality........	1	29.0	22	24.0	16	34.0	21
Substitutes........	1	34.5	23	21.0	14	48.0	28
Clan Feeling.......	4	41.0	24	40.5	24	41.5	25
Nobby............	2	42.5	25	47.5	28	37.5	23
Recommendation...	2	43.0	26	48.0	29	38.0	24
Social Superiority...	4	44.0	27	41.2	25	47.0	27
Imported..........	1	45.5	28	45.0	27	46.0	26
Beautifying........	3	45.8	29	43.0	26	48.7	29

averaged to give the result in the table. Since this number varies from 1 to 5 the reliability of the various measures is not uniform, but the method reduces to a certain extent the influence of the particular way in which one or other of the various appeals may have been expressed.

Columns 3 and 4 give the final averages and positions for the combined groups of 20 men and 20 women. The values range from 4.0 to 45.8, these numbers indicating the average position in the list of 50 possible places. The group of appeals, as a whole, falls into *three rather sharply defined sections,* the series breaking at values 15.2 and at 29.0, at which points there are wide gaps, which contrast with the gradual transitions of value within the groups. And these sections, moreover, correspond to qualitatively different groups of appeals.

(a) *In the first group,* with values ranging from 4.0 to 15.2, fall the appeals to health, cleanliness, scientific construction, economy of time, appetite, increase of efficiency, safety, durability, quality, modernity, and family affection. The general characteristic of these appeals is that they are *strictly relevant* in tone, describe the article precisely or point out some *specific value,* quality or "selling point" which it possesses.

STRENGTH OF INSTINCTS AND INTERESTS

(b) *In the second group,* with values ranging from 21.1 to 29.0, fall the appeals based on the general reputation, guarantee or assertion of the manufacturer, and on the set of specific and more or less social feelings and interests, such as sympathy for others (not family), courtesy, imitation, elegance, hospitality, sport, cheapness, etc. The characteristic of these appeals is that they *do not relevantly describe the article, but try to connect the article with some specific instinct or effective conception.* And these appeals are distinctly less personal, *more social,* than those of the first group.

(c) *In the third section,* with values ranging (with one exception) from 41.0 to 45.8, fall the rather vague appeals to avoid substitutes, to civic pride and clan feeling, social superiority, recommendation, the ideals of fashion and foreign origin, and finally the beautifying appeal. The chief characteristic of this group seems to be that while, as in the second group, *the statement is semi-irrelevant or incidental, the feeling appealed to is indeterminate and general.*

The only considerable sex differences, cases in which the difference in position is, say, 5 places or over, are on the appeals entitled *appetite, safety, nobby, family affection, sympathy, elegance* and

279

recommendation which are placed higher by the men and on *time saved, guarantee, medicinal, substitutes, efficiency, durability, quality* and *hospitality,* which are placed higher by the women.

In an interesting continuation of this experiment five professional advertising men arranged the series of appeals in an order, not as they appealed to them, personally, but *as they judged they would appeal to the general reader and consumer.* This was done in order to see how accurately the expert advertising man could judge the feelings of his audience. The final average order, as arranged by these five experts, was then compared with the orders as arranged by the 20 men and the 20 women. Several interesting points resulted from this comparison.

In the first place, the consumers find greater differences between the various appeals than do the business men. The total range of values, from best to poorest, for the consumers, was from 4 to 45.5. For the advertising men the total range was only 11.8 to 40.3. This means that the advertising men did not fully realize the differences which were felt by the readers. To the advertising men the 50 appeals tend to be pretty much alike, or rather, these men believed that the consumers would feel the appeals to be pretty much

STRENGTH OF INSTINCTS AND INTERESTS

alike, in persuasiveness. They failed to appreciate the real effects of rather small changes in their copy.

By proper statistical methods a figure can be obtained which will show the degree of correspondence between the arrangements by the various groups of people. When this is done, a coefficient of 100 per cent. means exact correspondence. One of —100 per cent. means just the reverse order in one case of that in the other. A coefficient of 0 per cent. means only a chance or accidental correspondence. Intermediate amounts indicate corresponding degrees of resemblance between the two arrangements. The coefficients for these experiments are as follows:

1. The 20 men and the 20 women agree closely with each other, giving a coefficient of correspondence of 63 per cent.
2. Two different arrangements, by the 20 women, show a very high degree of correspondence (90 per cent.).
3. The average order, as arranged by the advertising men, corresponded only slightly with the average order for the men and women combined. The coefficient is only 36 per cent. of resemblance.

PRINCIPLES OF APPEAL AND RESPONSE

4. When the advertising men arranged the appeals as they thought they would appeal to other men, the degree of correspondence was fairly high, the coefficient being 65 per cent.
5. When the advertising men arranged the appeals as they thought they would appeal to women, the correspondence was much less, the coefficient being only 41 per cent.

That is to say, these experts had very incorrect ideas as to the relative strength of these appeals for men and women in general (36 per cent.). In the case of men alone, their opinions were fairly correct (65 per cent.), while in the case of women the opinion of the experts was much less reliable (41 per cent.).

Taking the table as it stands, the various instincts and interests there represented stand in their order of strength in so far as they may serve as the basis of appeal in business transactions, regardless of the commodity concerned. But it is obvious that not all of these appeals can be used in the case of any single commodity. Thus "Appetizing Qualities" cannot apply to the sale of diamonds or shoes, nor could "Durability" be applied to the merchandising of food

STRENGTH OF INSTINCTS AND INTERESTS

products. The table, nevertheless, affords an approximate statement of the relative strength of available appeals for any given commodity. It is only necessary to begin at the top of the list and select the first appeal which could be applied in the description of the commodity in question. This will then constitute the strongest appeal which can be made in the interest of that commodity. The next in the list which would apply appropriately would be the next strongest, etc. For example, the first appeal which would be appropriate to breakfast foods would be "Healthfulness." Then would come, in order of strength, as indicated by position in the table—"Cleanliness," "Appetizing Qualities," "Reputation of the Firm," "Medicinal Properties," "Economy," "Hospitality," "Substitutes," "Clan Loyalty," "Recommendation by others," and finally "Imported." If the reader will now turn back to the table in the preceding chapter, in which are given the results of a special study of the persuasiveness of advertisements used for breakfast foods, he will find that the order of strength of appeals as indicated by this abstract table coincides with the order determined upon independently by Strong.

PRINCIPLES OF APPEAL AND RESPONSE

SUMMARY

We may then summarize the practical results of this experiment under the following headings:

1. *The table of relative persuasiveness* affords a statement of the order of strengh, in general, of most of the appeals which can be utilized in the process of advertising and selling, regardless of the commodity concerned.

2. Selection from this table of the appeals appropriate to the description of any given commodity enables the formation of a smaller table in which the appropriate appeals stand in their order of relative persuasiveness.

3. Any sex differences, and the amount of these differences, may be determined by the comparison of the orders for men and women as given in the table.

4. The strongest appeals which can be made for any commodity, in the attempt to market it, distribute it, or secure publicity for it, will consist in strictly relevant statements of the characteristics, specific qualities or merits, or "selling points" possessed by the article. This will be especially true if these qualities take the form of cleanliness, healthfulness, scientific construction, economy of time, increase of efficiency, safety,

durability, modernity, appetizing quality, and the power to contribute to the welfare of one's family and dependants.

5. If a commodity possesses none of these qualities it is possible to resort to the use of a second but weaker type of appeal, by trying to associate the article with some specific instinct or effective habit of a more "social," less "personal" character than those of the first group, such appeals as those based on reputation of the firm, guarantee or assertion of the maker, sympathy for others (not in one's family), courtesy, imitation, elegance, hospitality, sport, cheapness, etc. These appeals are not descriptive of the article itself but attempt to utilize, in an incidental way, the strength of instincts and interests which are primarily concerned with situations outside the field of business transactions.

6. The semi-relevant or strictly incidental appeal, appealing to rather indeterminate and general interests, such as those based on civic pride and clan feeling, social superiority impulses, recommendation by others, ideals of fashion and of foreign origin, the promise of physical beauty, and the avoidance of substitutes, are the weakest appeals that could possibly be used. One

PRINCIPLES OF APPEAL AND RESPONSE

is amazed at the extent to which these feeble appeals are relied on in current advertising and selling, and is not surprised at the assertions of experts that two-thirds of the money devoted to securing publicity is wasted.

CHAPTER XV

SEX AND CLASS DIFFERENCES OF INTEREST TO BUSINESS MEN

I. SEX DIFFERENCES

It is not my purpose here to enter upon any discussion of sex or class differences in general, but rather to confine myself to such differences as have been experimentally shown to be present in the processes of purchasing goods, and particularly in the processes of reacting to the appeals of advertisements and of salesmen. Biologists have had much to say concerning elemental differences between the male and female reproductive cells, and have often reasoned, by way of analogy, and with insufficient caution, to similar or corresponding differences between men and women in mature life. The naturalists, in turn, have found characteristic differences in the organization and activities of the sexes among lower animals, and these differences have also been eagerly sought for in human society. The anthropologist has, in his own way, compared the activities and character-

PRINCIPLES OF APPEAL AND RESPONSE

istics of sex as these are reflected in primitive cultures, and many have attempted to trace continuities between these conditions and those of our own complex social organizations, institutions and activities. Finally, the experimental psychologist has investigated in great detail, but seldom with adequate accuracy or scope, the mental characteristics of men and women, as shown by their sensory acuity, their motor capacities, their imagery, memory, attention, associations, reasoning, feelings and emotions, suggestibility, interests, general information, activity, inclination, etc. Readers interested in the outcome of these studies may find them fully discussed in the books enumerated in the appendix.

In the present connection we shall ask but two questions, and shall seek to answer them in so far as this is possible in terms of our present knowledge. These questions are: Are there any characteristic differences between men and women, as we find them to-day, with respect to the ways in which they behave as purchasers of goods, or as readers of advertisements, or as auditors of selling talks? If so, the second question will then be: What are these differences, and can they be in any way specified, demonstrated and measured?

SEX AND CLASS DIFFERENCES

We may begin by inquiring whether or not there are characteristic differences between the things which men buy and those things of which women are purchasers? Clearly this is a question on which the practical business man should be able to speak with authority. But if he has ever formulated an answer to the question, he has either kept the data to himself or published them in inaccessible places. At least I have failed to find any account, in business literature, of what men and women buy. We must rely, then, for our information, on a preliminary study which I have made on a group of 25 New York City families, and must, of course, bear in mind that these results apply only to families of a similar type, living under similar conditions. How far a change in conditions effects a change in the rôle of men and women as purchasers only further investigation can reveal. But the present results are suggestive.

In this investigation members of the family were requested to report, with respect to 80 commonly used articles, whether each article was purchased (a) by the men of the household alone, or (b) solely by the women, or (c) by either or by both in consultation. Some information concerning the character of the homes included may be af-

PRINCIPLES OF APPEAL AND RESPONSE

forded by the facts that 72 per cent. of the families live in apartments, 60 per cent. of them possess neither vehicles of conveyance, pets, nor musical instruments. The annual income ranged

TABLE XVIII

Men and Women as Purchasers

Class of Article	No. of Specifications	Percentage by Men Alone	Percentage by Women Alone	Percentage by Both	Percentage by Neither
Men's clothing.	11	65	11	23	1
Women's clothing........	11	1	87	12	0
Druggist's articles........	6	10	48	41	1
Kitchen ware...	6	2	89	8	1
Pets..........	3	19	5	15	61
Dry Goods....	4	0	96	4	0
Vehicles.......	3	23	1	15	61
House furnishings.........	8	4	48	46	2
Musical instruments.......	5	13	7	20	60
Raw and market foods....	6	0	87	13	0
Package foods..	5	3	79	14	4
Miscellaneous..	12	6	22	68	4
Totals...	80	146	580	279	195

from $2,000 to $5,000, with perhaps a few running higher than this. The commodities may be classified under 12 chief headings, with a number of specifications arranged under each. The following table gives these general headings, with

SEX AND CLASS DIFFERENCES

the number of specifications under each, and the per cent. of the families which reported under the respective columns.

From the examination of the specific articles, the following interesting facts emerge:

1. The only article of clothing bought by men exclusively is their own collars. Only 80 per cent. buy their own shoes and hats. In over 50 per cent. of the cases the men's jewelry, handkerchiefs, socks, and underwear are purchased either by the women alone or in consultation with them. In one-third of the cases the women help buy the men's shirts. Only one-third of the men buy their own handkerchiefs.

2. On the other hand, the men participate but little in the purchase of the women's apparel. Women buy men's things exclusively 11 times as often as the men buy women's things exclusively. Women coöperate with men twice as much as men coöperate with women, in the purchase of their respective apparel.

3. In 100 per cent. of the cases women are sole purchasers of their own underwear, lace, thread, and cooking utensils. In 80 per cent. of the cases they are the sole purchasers of dresses, cloaks, footwear, hats, parasols, gloves, fans, handkerchiefs, clotheslines, chafing dishes, kitchen tables,

ribbons, cloth, flour, vegetables, eggs, butter, bread, cereals, water and canned goods. In over 50 per cent. of the cases they are the sole purchasers of curtains, mattresses, meats, ranges, talcums and perfumes. Women buy 83 per cent. of the food, but less than 50 per cent. of the house furnishings, exclusively.

4. Women buy more of the magazines, men more of the newspapers. Women buy many wedding presents exclusively, but men participate more largely in the purchase of Christmas gifts, birthday gifts, and children's toys. Only 5 per cent. of the pets are bought by women alone, 20 per cent. by men alone.

There are, then, considerable differences between the parts played by men and women as purchasers of goods. If there are now any differences in manner of reacting to the appeals of advertisements and salesmen, these differences will be worth knowing, and such knowledge might be effectively utilized in the direction and formation of appeals, according as they are designed to reach either or both classes. In the course of the preceding chapters there has frequently been occasion to refer to sex differences in one respect or another. These differences, along with others which have been brought out in experiments simi-

SEX AND CLASS DIFFERENCES

lar to those reported here, may now be brought together and confirmed.

1. In so far as we may rely on experiments which tend to show on the part of women a greater sensitivity to sensory impressions, and a more desultory and more permanent memory capacity, it is apparent that the mechanical incentives (intensity, magnitude, contrast, motion, isolation and position) will be less effective and more unnecessary when appealing to women than when appealing to men. Further, that there will be less need for devices calculated to fix impressions in consciousness.

2. Gale finds that women are more attracted by pictures than are men, and his curves of attention values of cuts and reading matter show genuine differences in this respect. Strong also finds that women are more attracted by cuts than are men. In discussing the results of a study of 50 advertisements for a well-known soap he remarks: "Only one among the advertisements preferred by women could be considered as approximating a 'copy-ad,' and there the main interest, apparently small, I should judge, would lie in the three small cuts." (p. 81.)

3. Much the same thing may be said for the use of color. Darwin believed that among the lower

animals the female is strongly affected by color, which the male consequently develops by the process of sexual selection. Thompson found that with the individuals studied by her, visual experience was more important in the consciousness of the women than in that of the men, and that only the women showed prominent associations connected with the different colors. In discussing the matter of color preferences we have already referred to Wissler's finding that the preferred color of an individual tends to shift toward the violet end of the spectrum as he grows older, and to the preference of men for blues and of women for reds. Of course these preferences are very dependent on the uses to which colors are to be put, and a preferred color for a necktie may not be agreeable to the same individual for the interior decoration of a room, or for the background of a billboard.

4. Gale reports that irrelevant material, whether in the reading matter or illustration of an advertisement, attracts the attention and consideration of women more easily than is the case with men. The table in which his data are given shows this to have been the case. Strong remarks, of his experimental results: "The preference for the irrelevant among women confirms

SEX AND CLASS DIFFERENCES

the early work of Gale upon attention value." (p. 80.)

5. With respect to the strength of special appeals, certain clear and interesting differences have been found. Thus in the table in the preceding chapter, giving the relative strength of a large number of appeals, the men may be compared with the women. The results of still other investigations make possible further such comparisons. Chief among the differences found here are the following:

(a) The appeal to civic pride, patriotism or other form of clan feeling is stronger with women than with men. In Table XVII the civic pride appeal ranks about the same for both men and women. But Strong found that advertisements for breakfast foods, based on the slogan "Patronize home industries," were rated "considerably higher by the women than by the men (11.1 as compared with 14.6) and that of the nine who ranked them above eighth place seven were women." (p. 45.)

(b) Appeals to authority of others and to recommendation by others are uniformly found to be rated higher by men than by women, although fairly low for both. Thus in Table XVII the "recommendation" appeals average position 38

PRINCIPLES OF APPEAL AND RESPONSE

in a series of 50, for men, and only 48th place in the series, for women. Similarly Strong finds that "authority advertisements appeal more to men than to women." (p. 41.)

(c) Detailed examination of the relative merit of the various appeals discloses the fact that the *women agree with each other* more closely on *personal* appeals (those based on such conceptions as "style," "nobby," "sanitary," "appetizing," "social standing," "time saved," "safety," "durability," etc.) than do the men. They agree with each other about 25 per cent. more closely than do the men. Furthermore, they agree in placing these appeals *higher* than do the men.

(d) On appeals made to the instincts and impulses underlying social solidarity, such as the recommendation, the reputation of the firm, family affection, guarantee, union made, sympathy, growth of the business, etc., the women disagree more than do the men.

(e) Men disagree most of all on the strength of purely *personal* appeals, such as those indicated by the words: health, social standing, efficiency, time saved, ambition, progress, competition, etc. Women disagree most of all among themselves on the appeals indicated by such words as popularity, recommendation, reputation, family affection, guarantee, union made, sympathy, growth of the firm, etc.

(f) These facts lead to the further generalization that the men are homogeneous, that is, tend to resemble each other more closely, on their *preferences,* on appeals which are strong. Women, on the contrary, tend to be alike with respect to their *dislikes,* appeals which are weak. Whether this difference bears in the direction of selection and difference in sex experience and training, or merely toward the temporary motives which operate in reacting toward appeals made in the interest of articles of commerce, the experiment does not show. The fact that women have definite and mutual *aversions,* with fewer common *preferences,* while men have fewer determinate *dislikes,* but definite and mutual *preferences,* is an exceedingly interesting discovery, and one which, if verified, may be found to have countless applications in business and in other forms of daily activity. Whether the difference be interpreted to mean a fundamental and inherent sex difference, or merely a difference which reflects our present social organization (which is doubtless an adequate explanation of all the facts) has nothing to do with the present usefulness of the fact itself.

PRINCIPLES OF APPEAL AND RESPONSE

It should be further pointed out that these comparisons do not rest on the results of a single experiment. Thus Strong finds that "when women are given an equal opportunity with men to rate appeals (advertisements) they are able to classify their dislikes as well as their preferences, which men do not. . . . A careful analysis of the data shows that women have more and greater dislikes than men, and are surer of them." (p. 79.) Further evidence is afforded by Kuper's experiments, described in one of the following sections of this chapter.

6. A final difference which is quite commonly held to exist between the ways in which men and women react to appeals has to do with the two forms of appeal which we have characterized as "the long circuit" and "the short circuit." Women are popularly supposed to react more strongly to emotional situations than do men. Since reaction to an emotional situation is what characterizes the "short circuit" process of appeal and response, this would be equivalent to saying that short circuit appeals, such as we have previously described and illustrated, may be directed to women more effectively than to men. Thus Scott says, in a description of the various ways of reaching a decision: "The woman's

method of decision" has characteristics of its own. "Insufficient time is given to the deliberation, or difficulty is found in classifying the problem. The deliberation is interrupted by a sudden extreme feeling of value attaching itself to one or the other contemplated alternative. The feelings rush in and take the place of reason. In deciding by the woman's method we are scarcely able to see how we reached our conclusion and we often speak of such decisions as being intuitive. . . . Women are supposed to decide in this way more often than men. They are supposed to have more perfectly developed instincts or intuitions. Their sentiment vanquishes attempts to utilize sophisticated reasoning and the outcome is frequently wise and in every way as worthy of respect as are the results of more complete forms of deliberation." (Scott, "Influencing Men in Business.")

The same writer then quite properly points out that "this method is not at all confined to women, but is a very common method of deciding any question in which feelings and emotions are prominent." Indeed, the present writer is inclined to go still further and to question the popular notion that women are prone to react more strongly to emotional situations than are men. The real difference, if any exists, is probably due rather to the *kind of reaction* which is made, and to the *type of situation* which experientially or conventionally has come to have emotional value. It may, indeed, be said that all of us reach our most important decisions through *feelings of value,* rather than by manipulation of logical premises.

II. AGE AND CLASS DIFFERENCES

On these points there is even less to be said than on the preceding topic. This is not because the differences are smaller, for none of the sex differences found are enormous, nor are they true of all individuals—they are differences between averages, and hold, when present at all, only of men and women in the long run. But the chief reason for the lack of material on age and class differences in reactions to appeals lies in the fact that the topic has seldom been investigated by precise and quantitative methods. An interesting study of the interests of children has been made by Miss Gertrude M. Kuper, who studied the reactions and preferences of 200 children of five nationalities, there being in the group 10 boys and 10 girls for each age from 6.5 to 16.5 years. The following results are quoted from a report of her investigation (*Jour. of Phil.,* July 4, 1912, pp. 376-379).

SEX AND CLASS DIFFERENCES

"The formal experiment consisted in asking an individual child to arrange nine pictures in the order in which he liked them best. The nine pictures were chosen to represent nine specific appeals: landscape, children, animals, religion, pathos, sentiment, patriotism, heroism and action. (They were Cosmos prints and therefore of uniform size and finish.) In all there were three series of these pictures each parallel so far as possible with the other two in their appeals.

"The results were tabulated according to age differences, broad social distinctions, and nationality, but in the last named case the number of subjects was so limited (10 boys and 10 girls to each of the following nationalities: Irish, French, German, and Italian, and only 9 girls and 8 boys to the Spanish) that the results are not held as significant.

"The positive data showed a sex difference in the order of preference for these several appeals. The girls' order was:

        Religion
        Patriotism
        Children
        Pathos
        Animals

PRINCIPLES OF APPEAL AND RESPONSE

>Sentiment
>Landscape
>The Heroic
>Action

"The last two were decidedly lowest in the scale and the first three were quite clearly highest for all ages; but the picture representing these nine curves was one of bewildering intersections as the values changed from year to year.

"The boys' order was:

>Religion
>Patriotism
>Action
>The Heroic
>Pathos
>Animals
>Sentiment
>Landscape
>Children

"The boys' chart representing the curves for these appeals showed greater agreement from year to year. Religion and patriotism, the heroic and action, and landscape and children, kept rather parallel courses all along the age scale, and no very decided tendencies appeared with

SEX AND CLASS DIFFERENCES

progressive age differences. Girls seemed to lose somewhat in interest in children and animals and to take greater interest in the heroic and action pictures. The latter change is explained by the fact that as the girls increased in school knowledge they read an historical background into these more or less warlike scenes.

"Another sex difference noted was *the number of positive dislikes* expressed by each sex. The girls gave 161 dislikes as against the boys' 65. Boys seemed to entertain relative indifference toward the appeals at the bottom of the list.

"In all their comments the girls were far more *personal* than the boys. The personal pronoun and references to their individual experiences were the usual preface to their statements. With the boys it was quite otherwise; they discussed the picture as an objective thing . . ."

These results are particularly interesting as indicating the early age at which appear the differences already discussed in the case of adult men and women.

With respect to class differences, the only experimental data known to me are those secured by Strong, who studied (1) a group of 101 educated business men, students and teachers, (2) a group of 95 educated women, and (3) a miscellaneous group of 97 men selected at random, and including business men, doctors, blacksmiths, storekeepers, saloonkeepers, policemen, bakers, lawyers, postmasters, etc. His report gives separate results for the groups men students, women students, farmers, business men, doctors, and miscellaneous men.

The only significant class difference revealed is to be found when educated classes are compared with uneducated classes. The difference then disclosed is suggested in the remark: "It may be that this is a characteristic of such a group of uneducated persons—that they are unable to differentiate complex appeals. That is to say, that on the whole any one of these appeals is as strong as any other . . ." Strong further shows that in experiments intended to measure the relative strength of these appeals, whether for psychological or for practical purposes, "A group of 50 college students will represent very closely the judgment of groups of educated men and women, of young business men, such as attend evening school, etc. They will not represent at all the judgment of groups from small towns and farming sections such as regions around Garrison, N. Y., from which the data were obtained." (p. 62.)

SEX AND CLASS DIFFERENCES

By way of conclusion it may be remarked that, although most of the results presented in this treatment of the principles of appeal and response have been demonstrated to be completely valid, many of them must be held to be rather suggestive than proved. They should be suggestive in the first place of the kind of information that may be secured when human nature is submitted to experiment for the purpose of securing more knowledge for the concrete purposes of practical living. They should be further suggestive of at least some of the methods which may be profitably adopted in such experiments. At most, it is not so much the possession of psychological data which will prove of practical service in daily life, but rather the acquisition of the psychological attitude of inquiry, observation and interpretation. In the opinion of the writer the actual *content* of this book will prove of less ultimate service than the *method* which it advocates —that method being in the long run the method which must be adopted by any psychological inquiry which aspires to be fruitful, the method of systematically observing, analysing and formulating *the way in which the mind works,* rather than *what is in the mind* as its work proceeds.

BOOKS AND ARTICLES REFERRED TO IN THE TEXT OR RECOMMENDED FOR FURTHER READING

CHAPTER I

ADVERTISING MAGAZINES. Advertising and Selling, Judicious Advertising, Printer's Ink, etc. Articles on Replies, Sales, Keying Copy, etc.

HOLLINGWORTH. Judgments of Persuasiveness. (Psych. Rev., 1911.)

STRONG, E. K., Jr. The Relative Merits of Advertising. (Arch. Psychol.)

YERKES. Article in Jour. Ed. Psychol., 1911.

CHAPTER II

JAMES. Principles of Psychology.
LADD AND WOODWORTH. Physiological Psychology.
PILLSBURY. Essentials of Psychology.
THORNDIKE. Elements of Psychology.

CHAPTER III

CALKINS AND HOLDEN. Modern Advertising. (Appletons.)
DEWEESE. Practical Publicity.
FRENCH. Science and Art of Advertising.
KENNEDY. Intensive Advertising. Reason-Why Advertising.
LEWIS. Financial Advertising.
MATAJA. *Die Reklame.*
STARCH. Principles of Advertising.

REFERENCES FOR FURTHER READING

CHAPTER IV

ARNOLD. Attention and Interest.
PILLSBURY. Attention.
RIBOT. Diseases of Attention.
TITCHENER. Text Book of Psychology.

CHAPTER V

HUEY. Physiology and Psychology of Reading.
MÜNSTERBERG. Psychology and Industrial Efficiency.
ROETHLEIN. Article in Amer. Jour. Psychol., 1912.
SCOTT. Psychology of Advertising. Theory of Advertising.
STRONG. Research Bulletins of New York Advertising Men's League.

CHAPTERS VI AND VII

ALLEN. Physiological Æsthetics.
GALE. Psychology of Advertising. (Minnesota Studies.)
HOLLINGWORTH. Judgments of the Comic. (Psych. Rev., 1911.)
LE CONTE. Sight.
RICE. Visual Acuity with Lights of Different Colors. (Arch. Psychol.)
STRONG. Relative Merits of Advertisements. (Arch. Psychol.)

CHAPTERS VIII AND IX

ALLEN. Physiological Æsthetics.
GORDON. Æsthetics.
HOLLINGWORTH. Obliviscence of the Disagreeable. (Jour. Phil., 1910.)

PARSONS. Principles of Advertising Arrangement. (Published by the Prang Co. for the New York Advertising Men's League.)

PUFFER. Psychology of Beauty.

CHAPTER X

GALTON. Inquiries into Human Faculty.

GORDON. Æsthetics.

PARSONS. Principles of Advertising Arrangement.

SCOTT. Psychology of Advertising. Theory of Advertising.

SHERMAN. Elements of Literature.

TITCHENER. Text Book of Psychology.

CHAPTER XI

BEAN. The Curve of Forgetting. (Arch. Psychol.)

CALKINS. Association. (Psych. Rev. Mon.)

DEWEY. How We Think.

EBBINGHAUS. On Memory.

LADD AND WOODWORTH. Physiological Psychology.

MILLER. Psychology of Thinking.

MÜNSTERBERG. On the Witness Stand.

SCOTT. Theory of Advertising.

WATT. Economy and Training of Memory.

CHAPTER XII

JAMES. Principles of Psychology.

MÜNSTERBERG. Psychotherapy. Psychology and the Market Place. (McClure's.)

ROSS. Social Psychology.

SCOTT. Influencing Men in Business.

SIDIS. Suggestion.

TARDE. Imitation.

REFERENCES FOR FURTHER READING

CHAPTER XIII

McDougall. Social Psychology.

Scott. Psychology of Advertising. Theory of Advertising.

Strong. Relative Merits of Advertisements. (Arch. Psychol.)

Thorndike. Elements of Psychology.

CHAPTER XIV

Hollingworth. Judgments of Persuasiveness. (Psych. Rev., 1911.)

Strong. Relative Merits of Advertisements. (Arch. Psychol.)

Wells. On the Variability of Individual Judgment. (In *Essays in Honor of William James.*)

CHAPTER XV

Boas. The Mind of Primitive Man.

Ellis. Man and Woman.

Hall. Adolescence.

Kuper. Interests of Children. (Jour. Phil., 1912.)

Ross. Social Control.

Strong. Relative Merits of Advertisements. (Arch. Psychol.)

Thompson. Mental Traits of Sex.

Thorndike. Educational Psychology.

Woodworth. Race Differences in Mental Traits (Science, 1910.)

PRINCIPLES OF APPEAL AND RESPONSE

Abbreviations Used in Bibliography

Am. Jour. Psychol.—American Journal of Psychology. (Worcester, Mass.)

Arch. Psychol.—Archives of Psychology. (Columbia University, R. S. Woodworth, Editor.)

Jour. Ed. Psychol.—Journal of Educational Psychology.

Jour. Phil.—Journal of Philosophy, Psychology and Scientific Methods. (Columbia University.)

Psych. Rev.—Psychological Review. (Baltimore, Md.)

INDEX

Abbreviations, 310
Activity, 114
Adaptation, 48, 120
Age differences, 300
Appeal, measurements of, 253; nervous basis of, 18; varieties of, 261
Association, feeling tone and, 172; laws of, 191; meaning and basis of, 190
Atmosphere, 176
Attention, causes of, 51; definition of, 46; fluctuation of, 133; holding the, 132; laws of, 56, 133; results of, 52; suggestion and, 232
Attention value of: activity, 114; arrangement, 152; black and white, 77; color, 96; the comic, 119; complexity, 135; feeling tone, 138; forms, 149; instinct and habit, 125; intensity, 61; irrelevant material, 110; isolation, 78; lines, 142; magnitude, 64; media, 37; motion, 74; novelty, 92; pages, 83; pictures, 106; pointers and borders, 137; position, 80; trade marks, 213; type, 72; unity, 136; white space, 77

Backgrounds, 77, 187
Balance, 153, 164
Breakfast foods, 249

Children, interests of, 300
Chromatic aberration, 104
Circulars, 41
Class differences, 303
Classified advertisements, 32
Color, attention value of, 96; balance of, 194; combinations of, 162; feeling tone of, 158; influence of, 97; preferences in, 98; third dimension and, 103; uses of, 102
Comic appeals, adaptation to, 120; attention value of, 119; defects of, 120; experiments on, 125; varieties of, 121
Complexity, 135
Congruity, 198
Content, feeling tone of, 158
Contiguity, 197
Contrast, 76
Correlation of judgments, 281
Correspondence, 45
Curves, 147
Cuts, attention value of, 106; relevant and irrelevant, 110

311

INDEX

Design, 152
Devices for aiding memory, 205
Diagonal lines, 147
Differences, age, 300; class, 303; sex, 287
Diminishing returns, 67
Directories, 44
Disagreeable, obliviscence of the, 140
Disagreeable words, 171
Display advertisements, 35
Distance of colors, 103
Distribution of appeals, 203

Effective conceptions, 242
Electric light advertisements, 14
Equipment of store, 42
Error, sources of, 274
Experiments, with advertisements, 5, 210, 247, 258; with advertising men, 280; on attention, 57; on balance, 164; with children, 300; on class differences, 303; on color preferences, 98; on the comic, 120; with elements of design, 151, 156; on imagery, 168; on legibility, 72, 186; on magnitude, 64; with mechanical and interest incentives, 127; with pictures, 109; on preferred positions, 81; on pulling power, 247, 257; on purchasers, 289; on relevant and irrelevant material, 113; on suggested activity, 118; on suggestion, 229; with trade marks, 213; with weights, 253
Eye, acuity of, 97; chromatic aberration of, 104; movements of, 80, 148, 180

Feeling of value, 300
Feeling tone, basis of, 138; of colors, 158; of content, 158; of form, 142; imagination and, 168; of lines, 142; of pictures, 173; of words, 171
Fixing the impression, 189
Forgetting, curve of, 202; the disagreeable, 140
Form, feeling tone of, 142
Forward law, 192
Frequency, association and, 200; suggestion and, 234

Golden section, 150
Graphite advertisements, 69, 114

Habits and instincts, 241
Headlines, 58
Holding attention, 132
Horizontal lines, 145

Ideo-motor action, 219
Illustrations, 106
Imagination, 108, 168
Incentives, comparison of mechanical and interest, 127; interest, 91; mechanical, 60
Instincts, as basis of appeal, 25, 239; nature and origin

INDEX

of, 237; relative strength of, 253

Intensity, 61

Interest devices, 138

Interest incentives, 70, 90, 127

Interest, individual differences in, 293, 300; memory and, 235; varieties of, 50

Laws, of adaptation, 120; of association, 191; of attention, 56, 133; of balance, 154, 164; of color combination, 162; of feeling tone, 139; of psychophysics, 67; of reading, 80, 117, 137, 180; of resting point, 114; of suggestion, 218, 224

Legibility of type, 72, 77, 180

Lines, feeling tone of, 142

Long circuit appeals, 23, 246

Machinery advertisements, 6

Magazines, 40

Magnitude, 64

Measurement of appeals, 1, 5, 253

Mechanical devices, 60, 89, 127, 135

Media, 38

Memory, devices for aiding, 205; for different kinds of facts, 208; experiments on, 208, 210, 212, 235; loss of, 203

Men and women, as purchasers, 289; interests of, 293, 300

Methods of investigation, 85, 253, 305

Motion, 74, 114

Nervous system, 17, 20

News interest, 39, 225

Newspapers, 38

Novelties, 43

Novelty, 92

Oblongs, 150

Order of merit method, 254

Pages, value of, 83

Persuasion, 132

Persuasiveness, measurements of, 258; table of, 277

Pictures, 106, 110, 173, 294

Pleasantness, 139, 199

Pointers, 137

Position, 80

Preferences, for colors, 98; for position, 80

Principles, of arrangement, 140; of connection, 191; of revival, 200

Provoking the response, 216

Psychophysical law, 67

Publicity advertisements, 83

Pulling power, 2, 5, 127, 247

Quality, of advertisements, 65; and balance, 165; of colors, 158; of lines, 142

Reading habits, 80, 137, 180

Reading matter, 112, 211

Reasoning, 22, 27, 224, 278, 284

INDEX

References for further reading, 306
Relaxation, 177
Repetition, 204, 235
Response, 18, 216
Rhythm, 152, 206

Selling points, 120, 278
Sex differences, 287
Short circuit appeals, 24, 218, 245
Similarity, 197
Soap advertising, 13
Space, 64, 78
Spacing, 181
Squares, 150
Stability, 156
Strain, 177
Strength of instincts, 253
Substitutes, 174
Suggested activity, 114
Suggestion, 218, 224, 229
Symmetry, 153
Synæsthesia, 176

Tasks of an appeal, 28
Third dimension, 103
Trade marks, 212
Triangles, 149
Type, legibility of, 72, 180; appropriate use of, 166
Types of imagination, 108, 169

Unity, of advertisements, 136; complexity and, 135; methods of securing, 137; of sentences, 58

Verticals, 144
Vicarious sacrifices in advertising, 213
Vividness, 201

White space, 78
Words, 171

Titles in This Series

1.
Henry Foster Adams. Advertising and Its Mental Laws. 1916

2.
Advertising Research Foundation. Copy Testing. 1939

3.
Hugh E. Agnew. Outdoor Advertising. 1938

4.
Earnest Elmo Calkins. And Hearing Not: Annals of an Ad Man. 1946

5.
Earnest Elmo Calkins and Ralph Holden. Modern Advertising. 1905

6.
John Caples. Advertising Ideas: A Practical Guide to Methods That Make Advertisements Work. 1938

7.
Jean-Louis Chandon. A Comparative Study of Media Exposure Models. 1985

8.
Paul Terry Cherington. The Consumer Looks at Advertising. 1928

9.
C. Samuel Craig and Avijit Ghosh, editors. The Development of Media Models in Advertising: An Anthology of Classic Articles. 1985

10.
C. Samuel Craig and Brian Sternthal, editors. Repetition Effects Over the Years: An Anthology of Classic Articles. 1985

11.
John K. Crippen. Successful Direct-Mail Methods. 1936

12.
Ernest Dichter. The Strategy of Desire. 1960

13.
Ben Duffy. Advertising Media and Markets. 1939

14.
Warren Benson Dygert. Radio as an Advertising Medium. 1939

15.
Francis Reed Eldridge. Advertising and Selling Abroad. 1930

16.
J. George Frederick, editor. Masters of Advertising Copy: Principles and Practice of Copy Writing According to its Leading Practitioners. 1925

17.
George French. Advertising: The Social and Economic Problem. 1915

18.
Max A. Geller. Advertising at the Crossroads: Federal Regulation vs. Voluntary Controls. 1952

19.
Avijit Ghosh and C. Samuel Craig. The Relationship of Advertising Expenditures to Sales: An Anthology of Classic Articles. 1985

20.
Albert E. Haase. The Advertising Appropriation, How to Determine It and How to Administer It. 1931

21.
S. Roland Hall. The Advertising Handbook, 1921

22.
S. Roland Hall. Retail Advertising and Selling. 1924

23.
Harry Levi Hollingworth. Advertising and Selling: Principles of Appeal and Response. 1913

24.
Floyd Y. Keeler and Albert E. Haase. The Advertising Agency, Procedure and Practice. 1927

25.
H. J. Kenner. The Fight for Truth in Advertising. 1936

26.
Otto Kleppner. Advertising Procedure. 1925

27.
Harden Bryant Leachman. The Early Advertising Scene. 1949

28.
E. St. Elmo Lewis. Financial Advertising, for Commercial and Savings Banks, Trust, Title Insurance, and Safe Deposit Companies, Investment Houses. 1908

29.
R. Bigelow Lockwood. Industrial Advertising Copy. 1929

30.
D. B. Lucas and C. E. Benson. Psychology for Advertisers. 1930

31.
Darrell B. Lucas and Steuart H. Britt. Measuring Advertising Effectiveness. 1963

32.
Papers of the American Association of Advertising Agencies. 1927

33.
Printer's Ink. Fifty Years 1888–1938. 1938

34.
Jason Rogers. Building Newspaper Advertising. 1919

35.
George Presbury Rowell. Forty Years an Advertising Agent, 1865–1905. 1906

36.
Walter Dill Scott. The Theory of Advertising: A Simple Exposition of the Principles of Psychology in Their Relation to Successful Advertising. 1903

37.
Daniel Starch. Principles of Advertising. 1923

38.
Harry Tipper, George Burton Hotchkiss, Harry L. Hollingworth, and Frank Alvah Parsons. Advertising, Its Principles and Practices. 1915

39.
Roland S. Vaile. Economics of Advertising. 1927

40.
Helen Woodward. Through Many Windows. 1926